S·P·A·C·E·S

Solving Problems of Access to Careers in Engineering and Science

1234567890123456789012345678901234567890123456789012345678901234567890123456789012345678901234567890123456789012345678901234567890123456789012345678901234567890

Project Director: Sherry Fraser

CURRICULUM DEVELOPERS:
Jean Stenmark
Diane Downie
Helen Joseph
Alice Kaseberg
Carol Campbell
Kay Gilliland
Virginia Thompson

Principal Investigator: Robert Karplus
Program Director: Nancy Kreinberg
Evaluator: Elizabeth Stage
Assistant Evaluator: Darlene Clement

Contributors: Linda Bird, James Brown, Lucille Day, Judith Donoghue, Susan Dutcher, Coleman Feeney, Bill Hunter, Bobby Jensen, Rita Laherty, Irene Miura, Jody Murdoch, Helen Raymond, Diane Resek, Robbie Roberts, Flora Russ, Hal Saunders, Oscar Schaaf, Joan Skolnick, Paul Sollott, and Molly Whiteley

1234567890123456789012345678901234567890123456789012345678901234567890123456789012345678901234567890123456789012345678901234567890123456789012345678901234567890

Math and Career Activities for Elementary and Secondary Students

DALE
SEYMOUR
PUBLICATIONS
P.O. BOX 10888
PALO ALTO, CA 94303

1234567890123456789012345678901234567890123456789012345678901234567890123456789012345678901234567890123456789012345678901234567890

S P A C E S was developed by The Lawrence Hall of Science at the University of California, Berkeley. The Lawrence Hall of Science is a public science center, teacher training institution, and research unit in science education.

Credits
Design and Illustration: William S. Wells Inc.
Editorial Assistance: Kay Fairwell

Cover based on the quilt "Japanese Waves" by Susan M. Arnold

DALE
SEYMOUR
PUBLICATIONS
P.O. BOX 10888
PALO ALTO, CA 94303

DS07401
ISBN 0-86651-147-4
13 14 15 16 17 18 19 20 21-MA-95 94 93 92

Contents

1

DESIGN AND CONSTRUCTION

2

VISUALIZATION

3

TOOL ACTIVITIES

4

ATTITUDES AND PERSONAL GOALS

5

JOB REQUIREMENTS AND DESCRIPTIONS

6

WOMEN IN CAREERS

1234567890123456789012345678901234567890123456789012345678901234567890123456789012345678901234567890123456789012345678901234567890

	Activities — Grades 4–10	Logical Thinking	Spatial Visualization	Estimation	Research and Organization	Math Preparation	Career Awareness
1	**DESIGN AND CONSTRUCTION**						
	Lots of Room	●	●	●	●		
	Build the Highest Tower	●	●		●		
	Design a Veterinarian's Office	●	●	●	●		●
	Marble Shoot	●	●	●	●		
	Environmental Engineering	●	●	●	●		●
2	**VISUALIZATION**						
	The Traveling Engineer			●	●	●	●
	Sorting Circles	●	●		●		
	Flowcharting	●	●		●		
	It's All In How You Look At It	●	●		●		
3	**TOOL ACTIVITIES**						
	Sort-A-Tool	●	●		●		●
	Tool Vocabulary	●			●		●
	Toolin' Around	●	●				●
	Spaces Construction Company	●	●		●		●
4	**ATTITUDES AND PERSONAL GOALS**						
	Cooperative Logic	●		●	●	●	●
	Typical Day			●	●	●	●
	I'll Probably Be . . .	●	●		●		●
	Building a Schedule of Classes	●		●			
	Fear of Math—Fact or Fantasy?	●	●		●	●	
	This is Your Lifeline	●	●	●	●	●	●
	Math: What's It All About?					●	●
	Viewpoints					●	●
5	**JOB REQUIREMENTS AND DESCRIPTIONS**						
	Career Cards			●	●		●
	Who Am I?	●	●	●	●		●
	What's My Line?	●	●	●	●		●
	Plant Parenthood	●			●		●
	Do You Want To Be an Engineer?				●		●
	Going to the Workforce	●		●		●	●
	Math Used in Jobs	●		●		●	●
6	**WOMEN IN CAREERS**						
	Classify the Classified	●		●	●		●
	Startling Statements	●		●			●
	Who's Where in the Workforce	●	●	●	●		●
	Women Scientists	●			●		●

Preface

1234567890123456789012345678901234567890123456789012345678901234567890123456789012345678901234567890123456789012345678901234567890

Solving Problems of Access to Careers in Engineering and Science —SPACES—is a collection of activities designed to: stimulate students' thinking about scientific careers, develop problem solving skills, promote positive attitudes toward the study of mathematics, increase interest and knowledge about scientific work, strengthen spatial visualization skills, and introduce language and familiarity with mechanical tools.

These activities are a natural development from earlier work at the Lawrence Hall of Science (University of California, Berkeley). First came "Math for Girls," a course established in 1974 to increase the participation of six- to twelve-year-old girls in after-school mathematics courses offered at the Hall. The need for such a class arose from the recognition that college women were entering the University of California inadequately prepared in mathematics and were consequently unable to enter a majority of undergraduate majors that depended upon a minimum of three years of high school mathematics. In addition, girls represented less than 25% of students participating in math and science classes at the Hall, affirming our suspicions that the attrition of young women from mathematics begins at a very young age. Since 1974, nearly 1,000 girls have taken the course and the enrollment of girls in classes other than Math for Girls has risen to 38%. A book detailing the curriculum (*Math for Girls and Other Problem Solvers*) is available from the Lawrence Hall of Science.

In 1977, the Lawrence Hall established the EQUALS Teacher Education Program to assist classroom teachers, counselors, and administrators in attracting and retaining girls and young women in mathematics courses, thereby better preparing them to consider entering math-based fields of study and work.

In California, 1,500 educators have received from 10 to 30 hours of inservice instruction and another 2,000 educators in 25 other states have participated in the program. The publication, *Use EQUALS to Promote the Participation of Women in Mathematics,* details the inservice training and provides descriptions of many classroom activities.

Evaluation data indicate that, in secondary schools in which EQUALS has been working for two or more years, there is a slow, but steady, increase in the number of young women in advanced mathematics classes. Further, students of teachers participating in EQUALS demonstrate improved attitudes toward the study of mathematics and increased interest in math-related occupations.

Based upon the effectiveness of EQUALS and because of a large number of requests from educators for more classroom materials, we received a grant in 1979 from the National Science Foundation to develop classroom materials for grades four through ten that strengthen problem solving skills and increase students' awareness of the relationship of problem solving to scientific careers. Another important goal was to help students

5

become aware of the appropriateness of women's participation in science and to encourage older students to consider a science career as an option for themselves.

The SPACES activities were evaluated in nine California sites. Fourth- through tenth-grade students who used the SPACES materials made significant improvements, over a comparison group, on problem solving and spatial visualization abilities; on career interest and knowledge; and on identification of mechanical tools. These results indicate that we have accomplished what we set out to do, and the materials are now yours to use and adapt for your own purposes.

We are grateful to all of the people on the title page for contributing to the development and production of this project. We would also like to acknowledge the superb cooperation we received from our field site coordinators who supervised the testing of the materials and provided us with information to make revisions: Steve Abensohn and Kris Shaff, San Francisco Unified School District; Virginia Austin, Mt. Diablo Unified School District; Beverleen Clark, Sacramento City Unified School District; Roberta Davis, Oakland Unified School District; Delpha Fliegel and Vanessa Fujimoto, Richmond Unified School District; Nancy Hays, Berkeley Unified School District; Alice Kaseberg, Eugene (Oregon) Public Schools; Margaret Schuler, San Juan Unified School District; Molly Whiteley, Napa Unified School District; and the Novato Unified School District.

Nancy Kreinberg, Director
Math and Science Education for Women
Lawrence Hall of Science
April 1982

1234567890123456789012345678901234567890123456789012345678901234567890123456789012345678901234567890123456789012345678901234567890

SPACES is designed to involve students in a range of mathematics topics and to give them experience in developing logical reasoning and problem solving skills. The organizational chart on page 3 sets forth both the content and skill areas presented, as well as an approximate grade level guide.

You will find that your students will have an opportunity to collect and organize their own data and to learn more about occupations that have not been traditionally pursued by young women. They will also become involved in estimating, guessing, predicting, and creating mathematical or physical models—all of which are components of the scientific process.

Grade Levels

Although approximate grade levels are indicated in the organizational chart, the activities may be adapted or used as they are for a variety of grade levels and with all students. The information and skill development are equally useful for young men and women.

Organizational Categories

The categories into which the activities have been divided are:
• Design and Construction
• Visualization
• Tool Activities
• Attitudes and Personal Goals
• Job Requirements and Descriptions
• Women in Careers

Design and Construction

Planning ahead, visualizing different uses of space and materials, making model representations, working in groups—all of these are essential skills for most scientific or technical careers. In these activities, students explore architecture, engineering, drafting, and other occupations by designing and doing either a layout or a model of a room, a veterinarian's office, a park, a tower, or a marble shooter.

Visualization

Solutions to problems often are found through pictorial representations or through the construction of three-dimensional models. Sometimes, however, models cannot be constructed, in which case, the ability to analytically examine a visual representation of the problem is necessary. To develop this ability, students are given optical illusion surveys, flowcharting, attribute sorting, and measurement activities.

Tool Activities

These activities address the need of most female students to learn about the use of standard tools. The series includes vocabulary lists, sorting tools according to use, filling story blanks, and construction application simulations. To use these activities most effectively, it would be important for students to be able to see, feel, and use real tools. Field trips to construction sites and hardware stores, and classroom visits by tool-carrying role models, would be a valuable introduction or follow-up to the activities.

Attitudes and Personal Goals

In this section, students are given an opportunity to explore their feelings about mathematics and some of the careers in which they may be interested, while they develop problem solving skills. An example is *Typical Day:* Students describe their ideas about a typical day in the life of an adult in a specific job. Following this, they interview an adult who holds that job, to see whether their impressions match the facts. In another activity, students are asked to estimate the length of their own working life, as well as other events they imagine in their futures.

Job Requirements and Descriptions

This group of activities provides a variety of ways for the teacher to inform students about careers. Using definitions of math-based occupations, statistics about the mathematics required for entry into certain jobs, information about mathematics used on jobs, and a questionnaire about engineering characteristics, students become aware of the importance of mathematics to their future.

Women in Careers

Traditionally, young women assume that only men work in occupations such as science and engineering. The activities in this section present two kinds of information: histories of women who have pioneered in scientific and technical fields, and statistics showing how few women are presently in many of the occupations. The activities will help students understand the importance of taking as much mathematics as possible.

We would appreciate your comments about the activities and suggestions for future materials. Please contact us at:

SPACES
Lawrence Hall of Science
University of California
Berkeley, CA 94720
(415) 642-1823

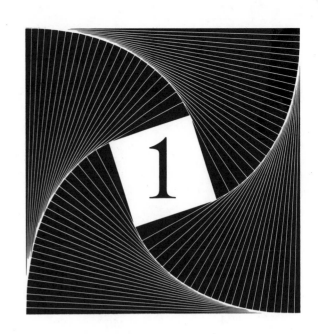

DESIGN AND CONSTRUCTION

Lots of Room
Build the Highest Tower
Design a Veterinarian's Office
Marble Shoot
Environmental Engineering

Lots of Room

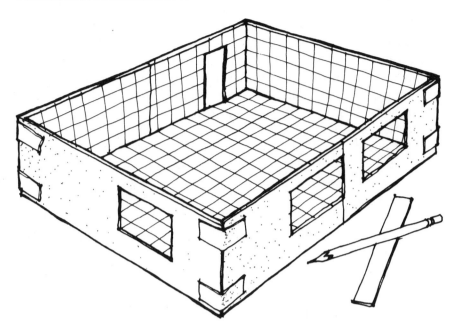

Skills
- *Estimating*
- *Metric measuring*
- *Scale drawing*
- *Constructing a model*

Time
- *1–2 class periods*

Participants
- *Groups of 3–5 students*

Materials
- *Meter sticks*
- *2-cm graph paper*
- *Masking tape*
- *Scissors*
- *Pencils*
- *Chalkboard*

Estimating, measuring, drawing and making a three-dimensional model of their classroom give students a feel for skills related to architecture.

Preparation:

Tape four sheets of 2-cm paper together to make one 17 × 22 cm piece for each group.

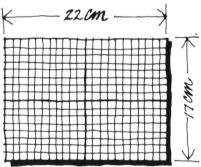

Directions:

Introduce careers that involve drawing and making models of rooms. Some of the occupations that might be mentioned are architect, drafter, decorator, engineer, and carpenter.

Estimate dimensions of the classroom. With the whole group, estimate in meters the length, width, and height of the room. Record on the chalkboard the guesses students make for each of these dimensions.

Measure the room. Divide students into small groups and give each group a meter stick, pencil, and paper. Have each group measure the length, width, and height of the classroom to the nearest meter. Groups will need to check measurements with each other. They will need to re-measure if they do not agree. Write the measurements on the chalkboard next to the estimates.

9

Make a three-dimensional model of the room. Give each group a large sheet of 2-cm graph paper. Each 2-cm on the graph paper will represent one meter in the room. Have each group lay out the length and width of the room near the center of the sheet of graph paper. Now they need to measure the height "up" the walls. Once the dimensions are drawn, the group can cut out their model of the room.

Add details. Each group can add doors, windows, and other features and decorate it as they wish. They may wish to fold up the walls without taping them yet, to see where the doors, windows, and wall decorations should go.

Fold up the walls of the room and tape them together. Have students find the areas of each wall and of the floor. What is the area of the ceiling?

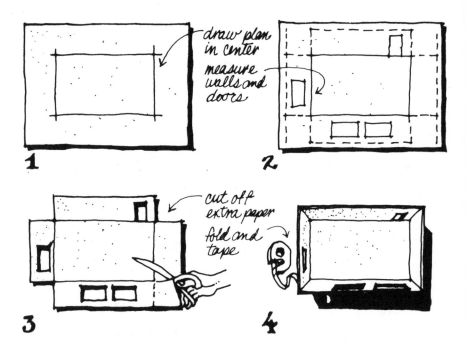

Note: If the floor and walls of the classroom are not rectangular, make a model of a room in the building that is rectangular.

Extensions:

1) Estimate the volume of the room. Have the students guess the number of 2-cm cubes necessary to fill their model. Record the guesses on the chalkboard.

2) Give each group a set of 2-cm cubes to check their guess. Point out the relationship between the number of layers of cubes, the number in each layer, and the volume.

Build the Highest Tower

12345678901234567890123456789012345678901234567890123456789012345678901234567890123456789012345678901234567890123456789012345678901234567890

Skills
- *Brainstorming*
- *Cooperating*

Time
- *1 class period*

Participants
- *Groups of 2–4 students*

Materials
- *8½" × 11" paper*
- *Paper clips*
- *Scissors*
- *Masking tape*
- *Marking pen*

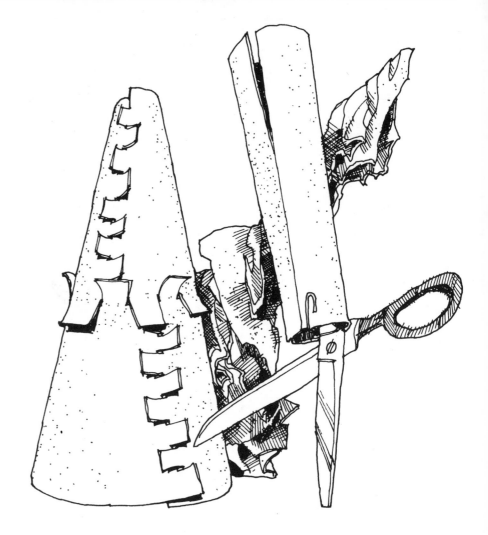

Students explore creative problem solving by using non-traditional materials to build a structure. The challenge is to build the highest tower using these materials.

Preparation:

1) Divide the materials into sets consisting of:

2 pieces of paper

10 paper clips

1 pair of scissors

You will need a set for each group of students.

2) Apply a strip of masking tape to a wall or door jamb starting at the floor and extending up about 5 feet. This will be used to compare the heights of the towers.

Directions:

Give these directions to the students:
• Only the materials provided may be used in building your tower.
• The towers must be free-standing. They may not lean against the wall or be held up.
• Towers must be brought to the tape on the wall for measuring. This means they will have to be transportable or easy to rebuild at the measuring site.

Divide the students into groups and assign a working area for each group of students. Distribute sets of materials and let the students start building.

Some questions may arise, such as, "Can we tear the paper?" or "Can the scissors be part of the structure?" The best response is to repeat the beginning instructions, without giving further information. The intent is to minimize instructions so students will be encouraged to invent innovative ways to build the tower.

As pairs of students finish their structures, have them bring the towers to the measuring site. Write the initials or names of students beside their tower's mark on the tape.

When all towers have been measured, announce the winners. You may want to discuss with the class some of the successful or not-so-successful strategies used to hold the towers together and upright.

Extensions:

Allow time for experimentation. Give the students 15 minutes to experiment with scratch paper before they actually begin building their tower.

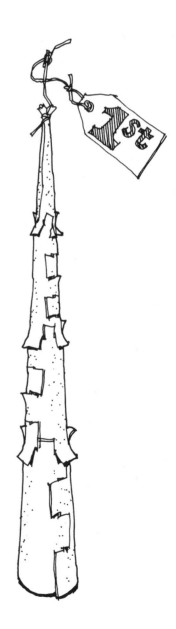

Design a Veterinarian's Office

1234567890123456789012345678901234567890123456789012345678901234567890123456789012345678901234567890123456789012345678901234567890

Skills
- *Metric measuring*
- *Estimating*
- *Visualizing spatial relationships*
- *Scale drawing*
- *Flowchart reading*

Time
- *2–3 class periods*

Participants
- *Individual*

Materials
- *Meter sticks or tapes*
- *Scissors*
- *Scotch tape*
- *Worksheets I and II; 1 of each for every student*
- *2-cm graph paper*

In designing a veterinarian's office, the students address problems faced by architects and engineers. Visualizing a fixed area based on classroom size lends reality to this spatial activity.

Directions:

Discuss the occupation of veterinarian with students. Have they ever visited a veterinarian's office? Do they know how a person becomes a veterinarian? Is there a difference between veterinarians who take care of large animals and those who take care of small animals?

Tell the students that their task will be to design an office for a veterinarian. The office space will be about the same size as their classroom. They will be given a list of equipment to be used in the office.

Give the students definitions of *scale drawing* and *floor plan*. A *scale drawing* shows the shape of something but in a different size. A map of California is a scale drawing. It shows the shape of California but is scaled down to a smaller size. The scale is always given: for instance, 1 inch could equal 100 miles. A *floor plan* is a scale drawing of a room seen from above.

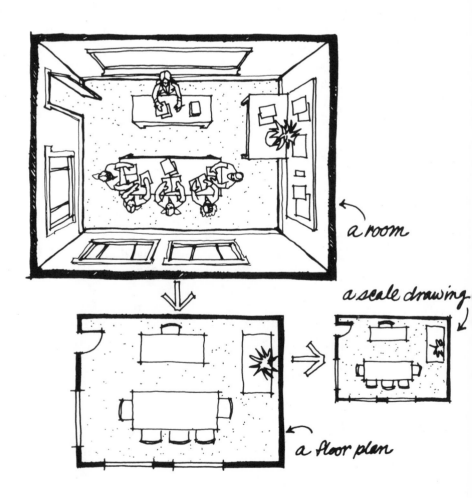

a room

a scale drawing

a floor plan

Show the students how to use graph paper to estimate the sizes of the equipment:

On a chalkboard or overhead projector, draw 2-cm graph paper lines as a guide for scale. Let each square represent 1 m × 1 m.

If a square is divided into 4 equal squares, the resulting little squares would be ½ m × ½ m (or 0.5 m × 0.5 m).

If the new little squares were divided into 4 equal squares, the new *tiny* squares would be ¼ m × ¼ m (or 0.25 m × 0.25 m).

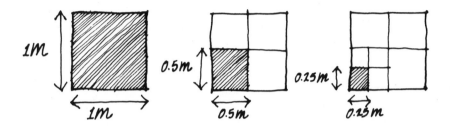

With this knowledge, the students can estimate very closely the size of scaled-down equipment.

Distribute copies of Worksheet I and do the practice scale drawing with the students. Keep the worksheet to use in the design of the veterinarian's office. (This is a good breaking point if you want to take more than one day to do the activity.)

Distribute copies of Worksheet II and 2-cm graph paper so the students can begin designing the office.

Extensions:

1) Using powdered chalk or white flour, lay out one or two plans to scale on the school grounds. Have students walk through the plans and critique the designs based on practicality.

2) Arrange a field trip to a veterinarian's office or schedule a veterinarian as a guest speaker. This is an opportunity to use a female role model.

3) Research the requirements for careers in engineering, architecture, and veterinary medicine. Possible resources are college catalogs and the *Occupational Outlook Handbook.*

Name:

SCALE MODELS

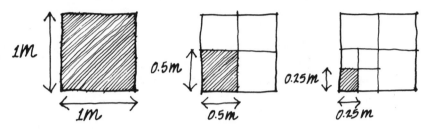

Use the diagrams above to help you shade in and label the following equipment on the grid at left:

1. Refrigerator (0.7m × 0.8m)
2. Sink (0.8m × 0.6m)
3. Examination table (0.8m × 1.5m)
4. Work counter (3m × 0.6m)
5. Desk (1.1m × 0.75m)
6. File cabinet (0.5m × 0.7m)

PRACTICE SCALE FLOOR PLAN

Design a laundry room in the space shown at right. First draw a floor plan, then shade in the washer, dryer, folding table, and laundry basket (circular).

1. Washer (1m × 1m)
2. Dryer (1m × 1m)
3. Folding table (1.3m × 0.6m)
4. Laundry basket (0.8m diameter)

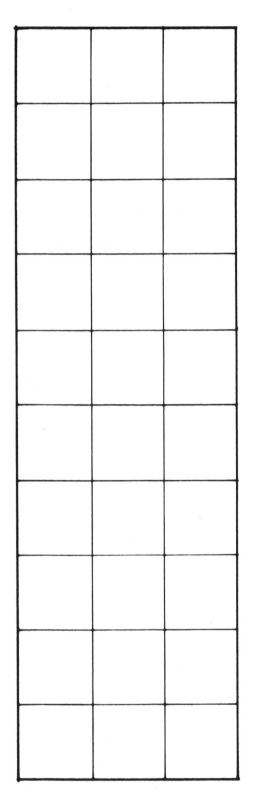

DESIGN A VETERINARIAN'S OFFICE Worksheet II

A young veterinarian is just beginning practice. By a strange coincidence she has rented office space exactly the same size as your classroom! She has leased (rented) equipment needed to start her veterinary practice. She needs your help! Please design her office.

EQUIPMENT LIST

Item	Size
Couch	0.8m × 2.2m
Desk	1.1m × 0.75m
3 Chairs	0.4m × 0.5m (each)
File cabinet	0.5m × 0.7m
2 Potted plants	0.4m diameter (each)
Examination table	1m × 2m
Examination table	0.8m × 1.5m
Sink	0.8m × 0.6m
Work counter	3m × 0.6m
Refrigerator	0.7m × 0.8m
Garbage can	0.6m diameter
6 Steel cages for for animals	1.2m × 0.9m

Note: The cages are 0.8m high and can be stacked to the ceiling. If the height of the ceiling in the vet's office is the same as in the classroom, how many cages can be put in one stack?

You can supply additional storage or equipment.

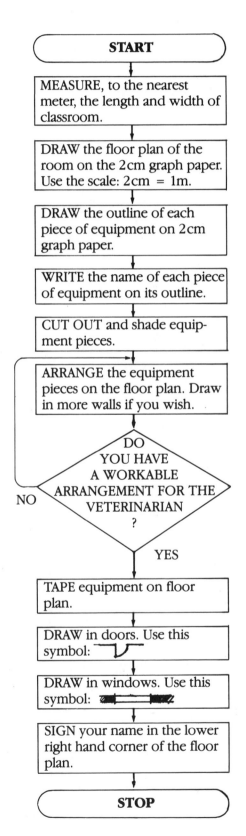

START

MEASURE, to the nearest meter, the length and width of classroom.

DRAW the floor plan of the room on the 2cm graph paper. Use the scale: 2cm = 1m.

DRAW the outline of each piece of equipment on 2cm graph paper.

WRITE the name of each piece of equipment on its outline.

CUT OUT and shade equipment pieces.

ARRANGE the equipment pieces on the floor plan. Draw in more walls if you wish.

DO YOU HAVE A WORKABLE ARRANGEMENT FOR THE VETERINARIAN ?

NO

YES

TAPE equipment on floor plan.

DRAW in doors. Use this symbol:

DRAW in windows. Use this symbol:

SIGN your name in the lower right hand corner of the floor plan.

STOP

2 CENTIMETER GRAPH PAPER

Marble Shoot

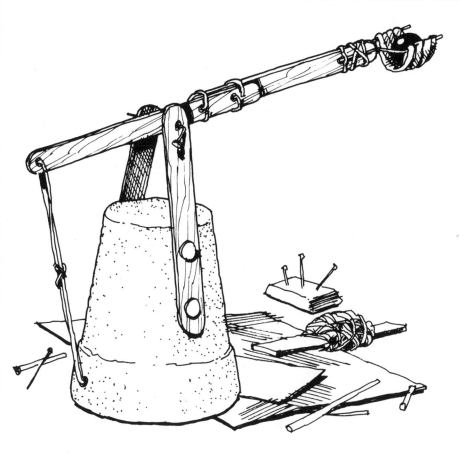

Skills
- *Cooperating with others*
- *Identifying trajectory action (catapult, lever, slingshot)*

Time
- *2 class periods*

Participants
- *Groups of 2 or 3 students*

Materials
(For each group of students)
- *2 rubber bands*
- *4 tongue depressors*
- *5 thumb tacks*
- *1 marble*
- *4 feet of string*
- *5 paper clips*
- *5 straight pins*
- *1 rubber eraser*
- *10 straws*
- *1 styrofoam or plastic cup*

Students use "junk" materials to build an instrument for shooting marbles or other small objects. This engineering problem is solved by experimenting with the physical properties of the materials and trying out different ideas.

Preparation:

1) Materials for each group may be pre-assembled in a large envelope, but the envelope may not be used as part of the shooter. Make sure all sets of materials are equal. For example, each group's rubber bands should be the same size, all straws should be the same length, etc.

2) Set up the launching pad, which may be:
- the surface of an upside down cardboard box,
- a line drawn on the sidewalk, or
- a book on the floor.

Directions:

The students work together in groups of two or three to see who can build the most effective marble shooter. *During the first class period* you may want to briefly discuss with students some different ways to move objects through the air.

"launching pads"

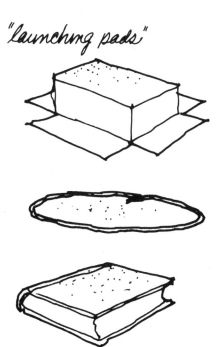

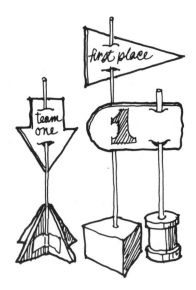

Read these directions to the students:

• Only the materials provided may be used.

• Scissors may be used to alter materials but not as part of the shooter.

• Operators may place shooters behind, on top of, or beside, but *not* in front of the launch pad. The shooter must touch the launch pad.

• When the machine is operated, the hand of the operator may go down or backward, but may not use a forward motion, nor move in the direction of flow of the marble (in other words, you can't throw the marble).

Distribute materials to the groups. Structures may be built during one class period and put into a safe place until the next class period.

During the second class period hold the Marble Shoot.

Set up the launching pad and give the following directions to the students:

• As each marble is shot, measure from the launch pad to the landing spot of the marble and mark the distance. (If the launching is held outdoors, straws with identifying flags can be stuck into the grass or dirt to mark each marble's landing spot. If indoors, masking tape can label the landing spots.)

• Members of the class may line up on the side of the landing strip to locate the landing spot since the marbles will roll after landing. The landing spot is the point where the marble *first* hits the ground.

• Each group will be allowed to shoot twice.

• A record will be kept of each group's best shot.

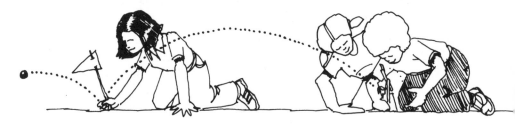

Extensions:

1) Make a graph of the distances.

2) Find the average of the distances of all shots.

3) Classify the shooters by the type of action, such as catapult, slingshot, lever. Find the average distance for each of those categories. Make a graph.

4) Allow students to redesign and perfect their machines. Have students make up a new list of possible materials for each group to use.

Environmental Engineering

1234567890123456789012345678901234567890123456789012345678901234567890123456789012345678901234567890123456789012345678901234567890

Planning ahead, considering use of space, working in groups, and making models are essential career skills. In this activity, the students explore architecture, engineering, and city planning through designing an environmental park in small groups.

Preparation:

1) Plan for student groups of three to four.

2) Cut one sheet of butcher paper for each group.

3) Duplicate student worksheets—one copy for each group.

Directions:

With the whole class, brainstorm a list of features they like in parks. You may want to talk about features other groups of people like—for example, what is needed for very small children? What about older people?

Present the problem. The size of the proposed park is 300 ft. by 200 ft. Compare this to some known landmark such as the school yard or a football field. Emphasize the difference between the required features (i.e. natural features: a hill and trees) and the optional features.

Put students in groups. Tables are helpful, but students may also work on the floor.

Distribute worksheets and materials.

Set a time limit for the students to come up with a plan they like and to draw these plans on paper. They may need to modify the designs to keep the total budget below the $5,000 limit. Allow each team 3–5 minutes to present their design and budget to the class at the end of the activity.

Extensions:

1) Take a field trip to a nearby park and sketch its layout.

2) Redesign the school playground.

3) Have students draw a park exactly to scale.

4) Make a three-dimensional model of the park.

5) Research the actual cost of materials and equipment to build your environmental park.

Skills
- *Organizing information*
- *Visualizing*
- *Group decision making*
- *Using models*
- *Estimating*
- *Computing*
- *Scale drawing*

Time
- *2–3 class periods*

Participants
- *Groups of 3 or 4 students*

Materials
- *Butcher paper cut to 3' × 2'*
- *Rulers*
- *Paper—plain or colored*
- *Crayons and felt pens*
- *Scissors*
- *Tape or glue*
- *Copies of student worksheets I and II for younger students*
- *Copies of student worksheets II and III for older students (7th grade and above)*

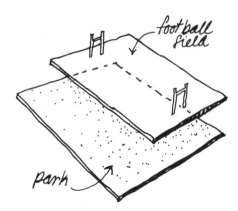

Let's assume that your town is going to change a vacant block into an environmental park and $5,000 has been set aside to develop it. The people of the town will do the work. Your class has been asked to design the park. Since the park will be for the whole community, you will need to include features that will be enjoyed by young children and adults, as well as by people your own age.

The vacant block:

The block is 300 feet by 200 feet.
It has:

- a hill
- two trees—one big and one little
- a stream

These features must be used, but you decide where to put them in your design.

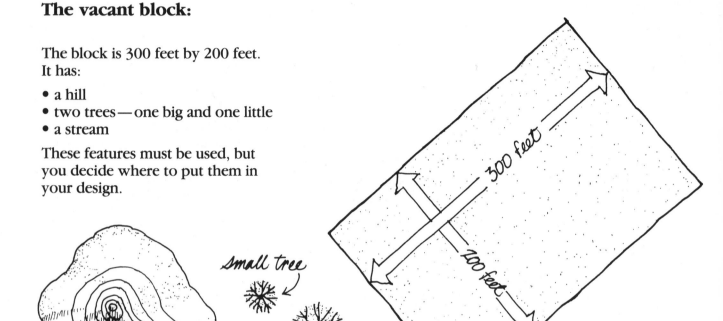

small tree

large tree

a hill

the vacant block

300 feet

200 feet

Your park:

Follow the steps listed below in making your design on butcher paper.

1. Write down materials and equipment (such as picnic tables) you want in your park.

2. Star (*) your favorite features on the list.

3. Look up prices for your materials. (See Worksheet II.) Remember that you get a hill and two trees free. If any items are not on the list, ask your teacher a way to find out the cost.

4. Draw in the natural hill, two trees, and the stream.

5. On a separate piece of paper, draw a picture of each feature and piece of equipment; cut out your pictures.

6. Experiment on the butcher paper with ways to arrange the features and equipment you want.

7. Find a layout or design you like that fits on the paper and costs no more than $5,000. Glue it down.

8. Present your design to the class.

COST OF MATERIALS AND EQUIPMENT

	Cost	Unit	Quantity	Total Cost
Rope	$1	per 10'		
Bricks	$1	each		
Sand	$1	cubic foot		
Stepping stones	$5	each		
Plants and shrubs	$10	each		
Trash barrels	$10	each		
Benches (6' long)	$15	each		
Old telephone poles (10' long)	$25	each		
Wire fencing (6' high)	$30	per 10 running feet		
Asphalt pavement (4' wide)	$40	per 10 running feet		
Picnic tables with two benches	$50	each		
Community garden plot and seedlings	$50	10' × 10'		
Animals　Small . . . .　Large	$20 $100	each each		
Drinking fountains	$75	each		
Pond	$100	each		
Playground equipment	$100	per item		
Bike racks	$150	each		
Barbeques	$150	each		
Street lights	$250	each		
Public telescope	$300	each		
Stage (20' square)	$300	each		
Bathrooms (one each, men and women) . . .	$350	pair		
Bleachers (grandstand)	$750	each		
Bridge	$1000	each		
Other (list)	$			
	$			

TOTAL COST: $_____

Spring Valley School District has decided to develop some of its land as an environmental park. Your engineering team has been asked to submit a proposal for the development of this land. Consider the following criteria when developing your plan:

Versatility:
• Is the park suitable for people of all ages?
• Can the park be used at night as well as during the day?
• Is the park useful in all seasons?
• Is there a wide range of activities available within the park?

Safety:
• How safe is the design for young and old users?
• Are there any possible hazards?

Aesthetics:
• Is the design pleasing?
• Would people of all ages enjoy the park?

Cost Effectiveness:
• Was the money well spent?
• Is energy used efficiently in the park?

Innovation:
• Is the design unusual?
• Are materials used in new and interesting ways?

Your team will choose a draftsperson, a finance officer, an engineer, and a public relations person. The major responsibilities will be:

Draftsperson: Draws design to scale and displays the finished design.

Engineer: Responsibile for design and safety.

Finance Officer: Keeps track of and presents the budget.

Public Relations Person: Keeps track of special features of the design and presents the team proposal. Prepares a five-sentence written summary of the proposal pointing out why this plan should be chosen over others.

The Problem

The area is 300 feet long and 200 feet wide (approximately the length of a football field and 1½ times as wide). The size of paper that you will use for your design is approximately 3′ by 2′. The area has the following natural features which must be included:

• 5 trees
• 1 hill
• an outcropping of rocks
• 1 stream

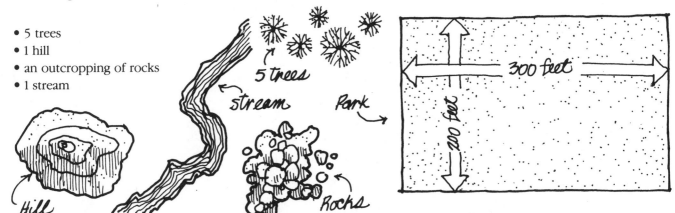

Your team decides where to put these natural features in your design. Worksheet II lists some possible materials and costs for the development of the land. You are free to use as much or as little of these as you wish. If you wish to use something that is not on the materials and equipment list, check with your teacher on whether the item is appropriate for an environmental park and what is the approximate cost. You have a budget of $5,000.

VISUALIZATION

The Traveling Engineer
Sorting Circles
Flowcharting
It's All In How You Look At It

The Traveling Engineer

1234567890123456789012345678901234567890123456789012345678901234567890123456789012345678901234567890123456789012345678901234567890

Skills
- *Metric measuring*
- *Drawing lines of a given length*
- *Map reading*

Time
- *30 minutes*

Participants
- *Groups of 2 or 3 students*

Materials
- *1 copy of Map Board for each student*
- *1 metric ruler for each student*
- *1 die for each group of 2 or 3 students*

The students use metric measurement to "visit" cities across the United States, simulating the travels of an engineer.

Directions:

Explain to the students that they are going to play a game in which they will pretend to be engineers who have to do a lot of traveling. They will be flying from city to city across the United States.

Divide the class into groups of 2 or 3 students, and distribute materials. Give the game rules as follows:
- Each player draws on his or her own Map Board.
- Each player in a group starts at a different city on the West Coast (Seattle, San Francisco, or Los Angeles).
- The object of the game is to visit as many cities as possible on the way to the East Coast.
- Players take turns rolling the die and drawing lines. The number on the die tells how many centimeters the player can travel on that turn.
- On each turn, the player measures and draws a straight line from the point where she or he landed on the last turn, to a new city that is as many centimeters away as the number on the die.

The player must land within the ring around the city, which is about 2 cm in diameter. If no city is within the proper range, the player loses that turn. For example: If the player who is at City A rolls a 5, he or she could travel from City A to City C, but not to City B, which is too close, or to City D, which is too far away. (It is helpful to demonstrate this on the chalkboard.)

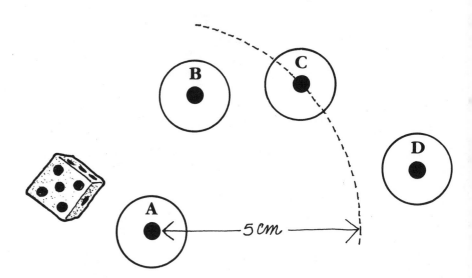

• Continue play until one player reaches Boston, New York, or Washington, D.C. The winner is the player who goes to the most cities without returning to any city already visited. Destination cities are shaded.

Optional rules or suggestions:
• You may (or may not) cross your path.
• You may start anywhere in each circle rather than from landing point.
• You may (or may not) turn corners on a single measurement.
• End the game after 15 turns.

Extensions:

1) Use a larger classroom map.

2) Add new cities, especially the city where your school is located.

3) Have several players use colored crayons and play on the same board.

4) Use a large map of your own state and make your own map board.

26

THE TRAVELING ENGINEER

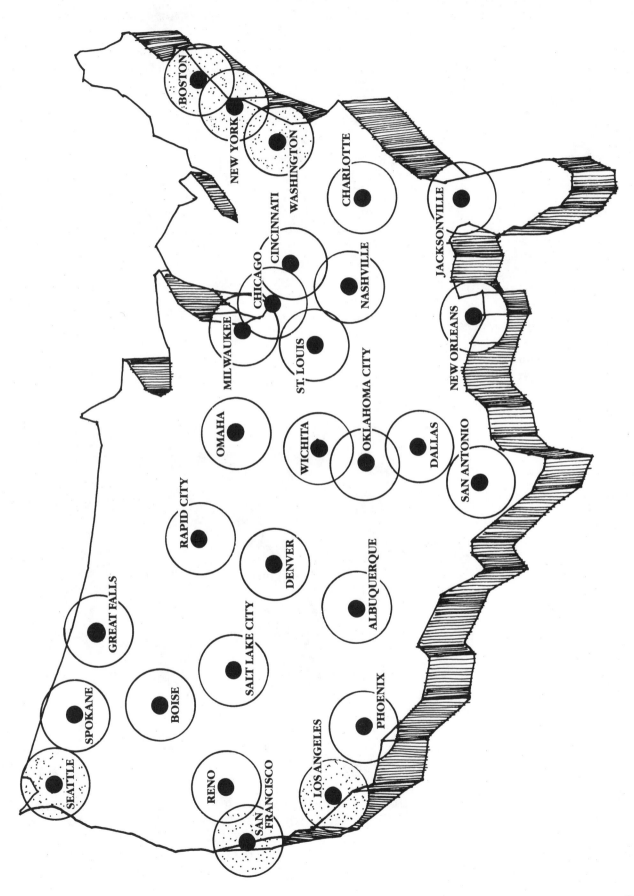

Sorting Circles

Skills
- *Recognizing characteristics*
- *Organizing information*
- *Logical reasoning*

Time
- *1 class period*

Participants
- *Groups of 2 students*

Materials
- *Copies of worksheets I, II, III and IV: one of each for each pair of students. If this is difficult, the diagrams may be drawn on the chalkboard and directions given verbally.*

This activity uses logical reasoning to classify objects according to important properties. Problems such as these often appear in college-level aptitude or achievement tests.

Directions:

Discuss with the students the usefulness of sorting and of classification systems. Some examples to mention are sorting mail by destination and identifying fossils by teeth.

Introduce "Sorting Circles" by drawing one large circle on the chalkboard. Label it "Things to Eat." Names of items that can be eaten belong inside this circle; everything else belongs outside the circle.

Inside the circle write the names of foods suggested by students. Ask where the word "spoon" would belong (outside the circle).

Draw another circle and label it "utensils." Spoon would belong in this circle. What else can be in this circle with the spoon? What belongs outside?

When students understand the idea of items belonging or not belonging in a given circle, introduce another kind of arrangement. Draw a large circle with a smaller circle inside. Everything that belongs in the inner circle also belongs in the larger circle.

With the students, identify some categories for the two circles. For example, fruit could go in the outer circle with berries in the inner circle. Are all berries fruits? Are all fruits berries? What would go in the outer circle but not in the inner circle?

Discuss the difference between the categories (circle labels) and the items that go into the categories. Worksheet I has categories in place and items are to be sorted. The other worksheets ask students to designate categories for a variety of circle arrangements.

Give each pair of students a copy of the worksheets. Encourage them to discuss the possible arrangements of each problem with each other.

Extensions:

If classifying objects is new to students, set up a learning center or class activity with physical sorting of buttons, keys, or other items in the classroom. These items can be sorted by attributes such as size, color, shape, or other easily seen characteristics.

References:

Marolda, Maria. *Attribute Games and Activities,* 1976. Creative Publications, P.O. Box 10328, Palo Alto, CA 94303.

SORTING CIRCLES

If you want to sort the buttons in a sewing kit into white ones and red ones, you might make two circles like this. Label one "white" and one "red."

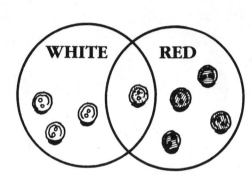

But then a button shows up that is partly red and partly white. So perhaps you could move the two circles together like this:

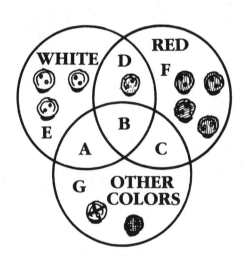

The next thing you know there are some green and purple buttons! We need a third circle for all those other colors. Label it "other colors."

Where would these buttons go: into section A, section B, or section C?
• A white and green button? _____
• A red and purple button? _____
• A red, white, and orange button? _____

Which letter is in each space?
• White only _____
• Red only _____
• No white and no red _____
• White and red only _____
• White and red and at least 1 other color _____
• White and at least 1 other color, but no red _____
• Red and at least 1 other color, but no white _____

SORTING CIRCLES

Two Sorting Circles

Here are some ways to arrange two sorting circles. Beside each arrangement is a list of words. Use these words to label the circles and rectangle.

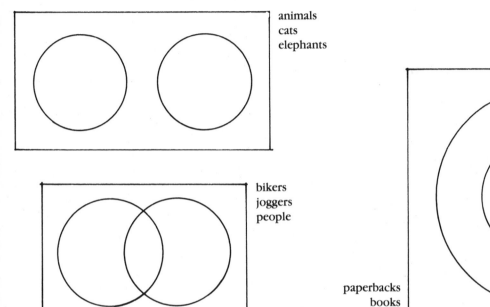

animals
cats
elephants

bikers
joggers
people

paperbacks
books
things to read

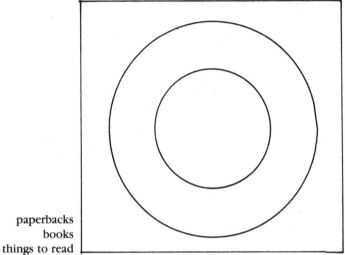

Match each list below with an arrangement of circles that fits. Label each circle and rectangle.

- **aunts, uncles, relatives**
- **soccer players, basketball players, athletes**
- **animals, birds, robins**

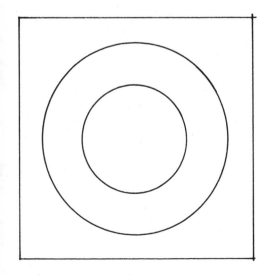

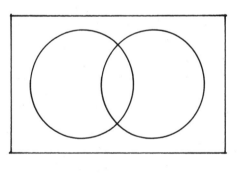

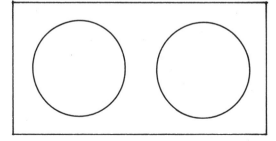

Three Sorting Circles

There are many ways to arrange three sorting circles. We have shown below some of these arrangements. Beside each group of circles is a list. Think about the items on the list and write each in the circle or rectangle where you think it belongs.

Here are some questions to ask yourself:

- **Which is the *biggest* group?**
- **Which is the *smallest* group?**
- **Is there a group that will include part of the others?**
- **Is there a group that will include all of the others?**
- **Which groups belong together?**
- **Is there a group that has no connection with any others?**

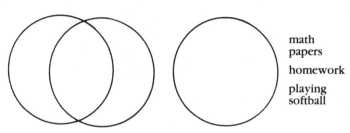

math
papers

homework

playing
softball

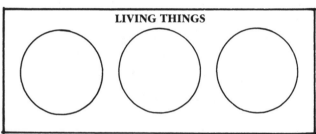

birds

frogs

plants

surgeons

nurses

doctors

medical
occupations

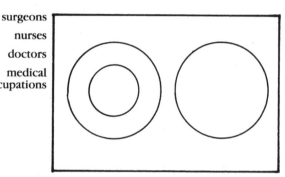

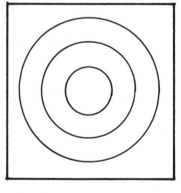

people who
travel

pilots

people who
fly in
airplanes

people

rocks in my
town

rocks in my
yard

gray rocks

rocks

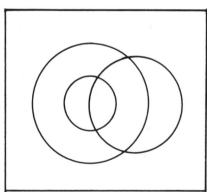

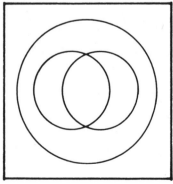

food

sandwiches

jelly
sandwiches

peanut
butter
sandwiches

brothers

computer
programmers

females

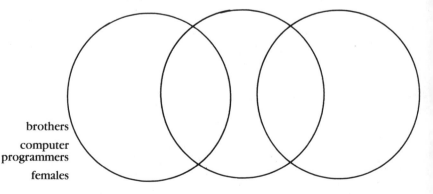

Sort Your Own Circles

Now try to make up some grouping circles of your own. Here are some categories to try:

1) fish, roses, flowers, living things

2) actors, painters, humans

3) flutes, wind instruments, sound makers

4) radio, entertainment, television, movies

5) sophomores, students, 8th graders, 8th grade girls

6) coins, dimes, nickels, quarters

7) timepieces, clocks, watches, stop watches

8) books, encyclopedias, novels, textbooks

9) Hawaiians, Americans, Earthlings

10) computer lovers, pizza lovers, people

11) sandals, boots, shoes

12) vehicles, cars, four-wheel vehicles, bicycles

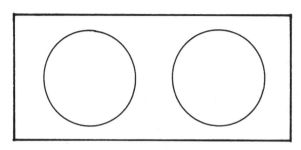

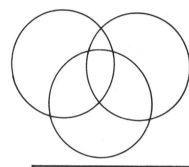

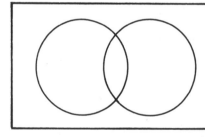

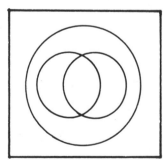

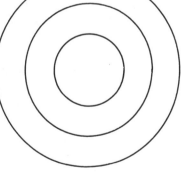

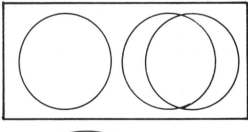

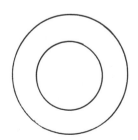

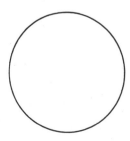

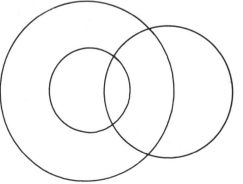

Flowcharting

1234567890123456789012345678901234567890123456789012345678901234567890123456789012345678901234567890123456789012345678901234567890

Skills
- *Creating step-by-step directions*
- *Learning flowchart symbols and usage*

Time
- *1–2 class periods*

Participants
- *Groups of 2 students*

Materials
- *3" × 5" cards or tagboard for making templates*
- *Scotch tape*
- *Rulers*
- *Scissors*

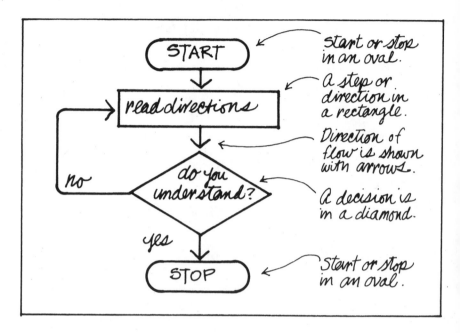

Flowcharting is useful in developing or interpreting clear and complete instructions. The use of standard symbols helps define the process of flowcharting. These skills are especially useful in computer-related fields, but they help clarify communications elsewhere, as well.

Directions:

Explain to the students the meaning of flowcharting (a way to give directions to a computer or a "robot") and the flowcharting symbols:

- **START** and **STOP:** The oval symbol is used at the beginning and at the end of a set of directions.
- **A STEP:** A rectangle indicates a step in the process or a direction. Some examples might be "Pick up the pencil," "Open your desk," or "Write 'HELLO'." A step has one or more paths going in and one path going out.
- **A DECISION:** The diamond represents a question or a decision to be made. A question should have only a yes or no answer. For example, the question "What color is it?" cannot be answered with a yes or no, but would have to be asked as a series of questions such as "Is it red?" and "Is it blue?" A decision has one path going in and two paths going out (one for "yes" and one for "no.")
- **DIRECTION OF FLOW:** The direction of the actions is shown by lines and arrows. The flow is usually down or to one side. Every rectangle and/or diamond is connected to other shapes in the chart.

Template

Each pair of students will need a template for drawing the flow-chart symbols. There are several options for templates:

1) Purchase commercial plastic templates.

2) Draw the template diagram on the chalkboard. Have students copy it onto 3″ × 5″ cards and follow the cutting directions.

template

3) Make a ditto of the template diagram and run off multiple copies onto tagboard for students to cut out.

Demonstrate the flowcharting of going out a door.

Write the following steps on the chalkboard:

START

stand up

walk to
nearest door

is door
open?

turn door knob

open door

walk through
open door

STOP

Answer Key

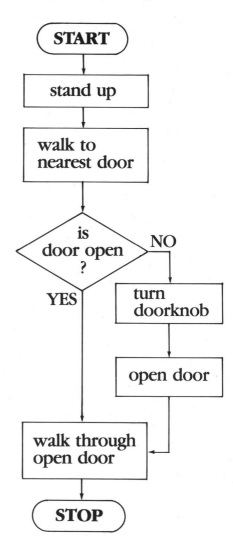

With the students, decide which symbol will be used with each step, and complete the flowchart as shown in answer key.

This is a good time to discuss some of the finer points of flow-charting with students. You may want to talk about the need for balance between thinking carefully about each step and being practical. For example, in the chart above, it would be possible to go to extremes and name each footstep and each hand motion, but that would serve no practical purpose in giving clear directions.

Have students work in pairs to make simple flowcharts of their own. Some possible activities which may be charted:

- Sharpening a pencil
- Putting on shoes and socks
- Buying a hot dog in the cafeteria
- Opening a window
- Going from one classroom to another
- Putting new staples in the stapler
- Making instant chocolate
- Hammering a nail
- Checking pressure in a tire
- Getting onto a bicycle
- Putting a letter into a mailbox

Extensions:

1) Have pairs of students trade flowcharts and check for accuracy.

2) Have students act out some of the activities they have charted. Are corrections or additions needed?

3) Have students flowchart an arithmetic operation.

FLOWCHARTING TEMPLATE DIAGRAM

CUTTING DIRECTIONS:

1) Cut out the shaded portion of each shape, leaving a hole of that shape in the card. (Hint: Fold the card down the middle, and cut out the shapes while the card is folded.)

2) Write the name for each symbol on the card above the shape (see diagram.)

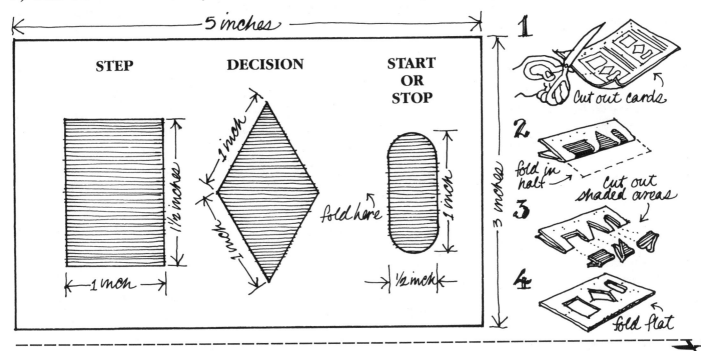

CUTTING DIRECTIONS:

1) Cut out the shaded portion of each shape, leaving a hole of that shape in the card. (Hint: Fold the card down the middle, and cut out the shapes while the card is folded.)

2) Write the name for each symbol on the card above the shape (see diagram).

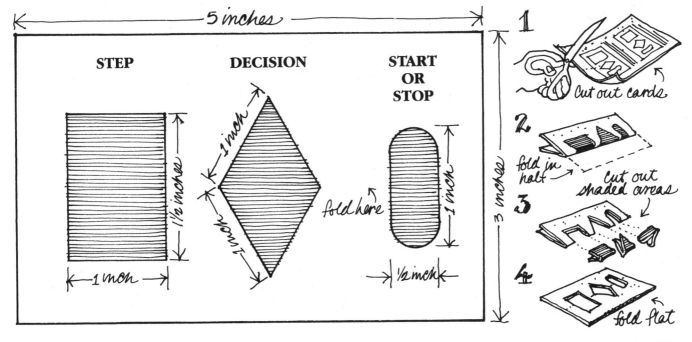

It's All in How You Look At It

Skills
- *Conducting surveys*
- *Organizing information*
- *Graphing*
- *Reporting data*
- *Visualizing figures*

Time
- *Explanation time: 15 minutes*
- *Research time: 1 week, outside of class*
- *Report time: 15 minutes*

Participants
- *Individual*

Materials
- *1 copy of "Picture and Record Sheet" for each student*

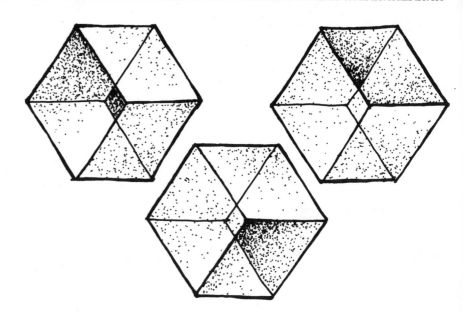

Making research decisions, conducting research by collecting and organizing information, and interpreting results are important skills for many scientific and technical occupations. This activity guides students through a research project that involves spatial visualization.

Directions:

Explain to the students that for the next week they will be conducting a survey among their friends and family on the different ways in which people see a shape.

Each student will have a copy of the "Picture and Record Sheet" to show to people and to use in recording their responses. Directions are on the sheet.

Before the students conduct the survey, they must decide which groups to survey. Two groups should be chosen that differ from each other in some way. All of the students in the class may use the same two groups, or each student may choose a different pair of groups.

Here are some possible pairs of groups to compare:

Group 1	Group 2
Boys	Girls
Adults	Students
7th graders	5th graders
Teachers	Parents
Basketball players	Nonbasketball players
Math class	Art class
Right-handed	Left-handed

Give each student a "Picture and Record Sheet." The picture should be shown, following the specific directions on the sheet, to at least 10 people in each of the groups (or a total of 20 people). Record the answers on the "Record" portion of the sheet.

When all the surveys have been completed, the students can post their results. If all the students have compared the same two groups, a large class graph can be made. Were there differences between the groups? Discuss the results with the class, concentrating especially on the steps of the research project.

Extensions:

1) Have the students find other optical illusions, or pictorial problem-solving acitvities. Make a class collection.

2) Conduct more surveys with the class's own picture set.

TALLY RECORD

Instructions:

Fold this sheet so that people can see only the illustration below. Write in the names of the two groups you are surveying. Before showing the picture to each person, ask that person to be sure to say the thing that first comes to mind. There will not be time to study the picture. Show the person the picture while you read aloud the question, "Which side of the cube are you looking into?" and then count 3 seconds. Be sure the picture is held straight in front of the person. Record the answer on the following Tally Record. Shade in a square in the appropriate row for each answer. Begin at the center line.

Shade in a square on this side of center for each person who says, "Left side."

Shade in a square on this side of center for each person who says, "Right side."

Name of Group 1:

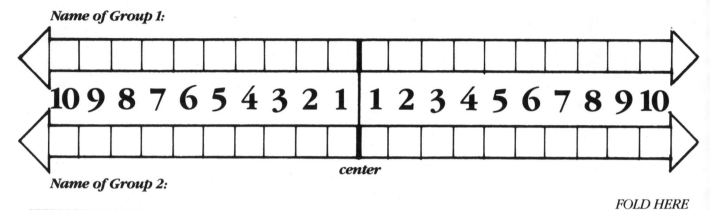

10 9 8 7 6 5 4 3 2 1 1 2 3 4 5 6 7 8 9 10

center

Name of Group 2:

FOLD HERE

RESEARCH PICTURE

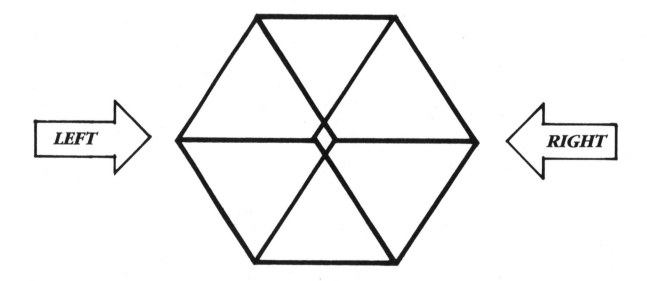

LEFT   RIGHT

Which side of the cube are you looking into?

3

TOOL ACTIVITIES

Sort-A-Tool
Tool Vocabulary
Toolin' Around
Spaces Construction Company

Sort-A-Tool

Skills
- *Organizing information about tools and their uses*

Time
- *1–2 class periods*

Participants
- *Groups of 2–4 students*

Materials
- *For each group of students:*
  2 yarn loops (1 meter long)
  1 set of tool cards (36)
  1 set of tool use cards (16)

Knowledge of tools and their uses can help broaden career perspectives, especially for young women. In this activity, students gain familiarity with the tools used in the construction trades and some understanding of the versatility of these tools.

Directions:

With the whole class, discuss the tools pictured on the *tool cards* and their uses. Write column headings on butcher paper, the chalkboard, or a bulletin board to show some possible categories of tool use, such as:

Cutting	Measuring
Pounding	Smoothing
Holding	Turning
Making holes	

Under each category heading have the students place pictures of tools used for that purpose or write in the names of the tools. Notice that some tools will belong under more than one heading. Tools not in the *tool cards* may be included.

This display of tools and their uses may be a useful student reference during the other tool activities.

Tool Sorting

Divide the class into groups of 2–4 students.

Distribute 2 yarn loops, *tool cards,* and *tool use cards* to each group.

Lay out the 2 yarn loops as illustrated:

Put one of the *tool use cards* in each loop. These labels indicate which tools belong in each loop. For example, any tool that cuts, such as a saw, belongs in the loop labeled "cutting." Any tool that does not cut belongs outside that loop (but may belong inside the other loop).

Divide the *tool cards* evenly among the students in the group. The students take turns, each placing a *tool card* where it belongs in the display. They should explain why each tool does or does not go in each loop. For example: "The vise holds a board but does not cut it."

This activity can be repeated with different *tool use* labels for the 2 loops.

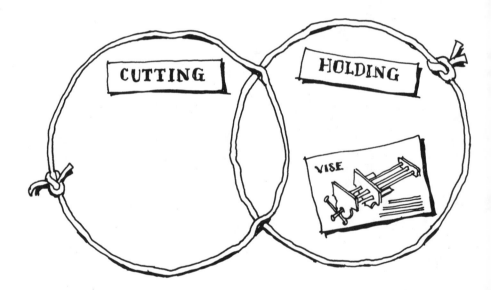

Extensions:

1) Younger students can start with a single loop.

2) Label the loops with *tool cards* and have students place the *tool use cards* where they would belong in the diagram.

3) Have the students draw additional tool cards. How many tools can the students find in the classroom? (Pictures of tools can be found in magazines or catalogs.)

4) Use 3 loops for these activities.

POUNDING	**CUTTING**
PRYING	**SMOOTHING**
MAKING HOLES	**CARRYING**
LEVELING	**LIFTING**
MEASURING	**TURNING SCREWS**
TWISTING	**HOLDING THINGS**
PULLING	**CLEANING**
FASTENING	**RECORDING**

Slip-joint pliers

grips, pulls, or turns hard objects

Long-nosed pliers

pinches, twists, and cuts wires and other small objects

Adjustable wrench

turns or holds nuts, bolts, or pipes

Chisel

chips, trims, and smooths wood

Razor knife

slices, trims, and cuts pliable materials

Linoleum knife

slices, trims, and cuts stiff (but not hard) materials

Any tool you want

Any tool you want

Putty knife

applies, spreads, and smooths pastes

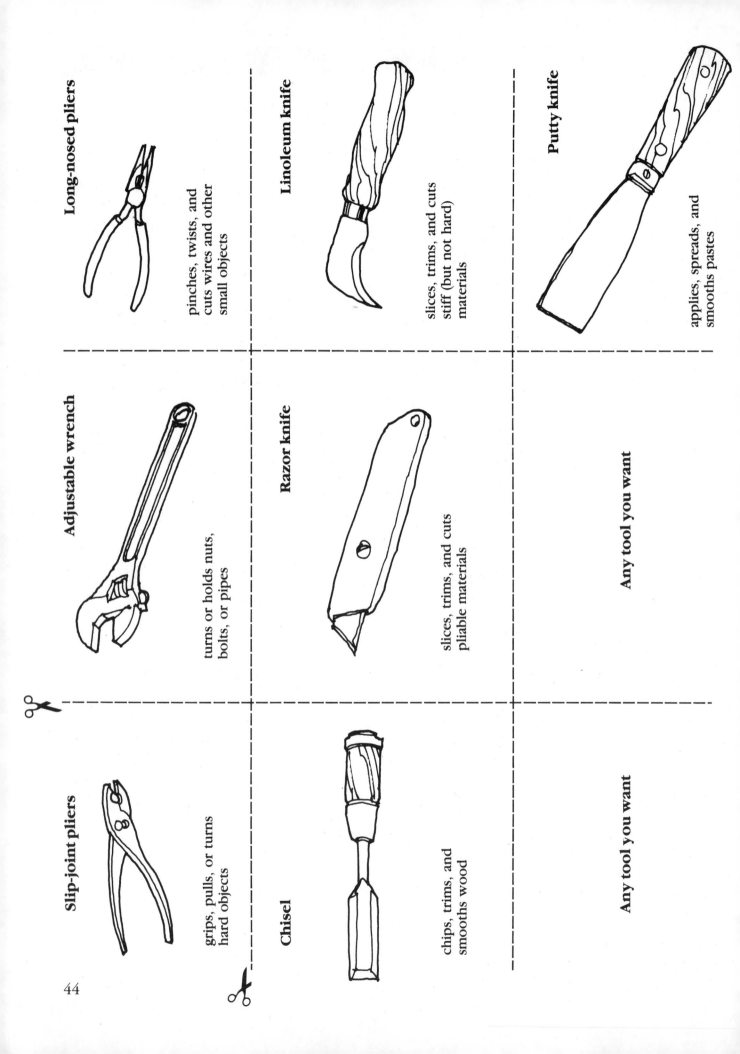

44

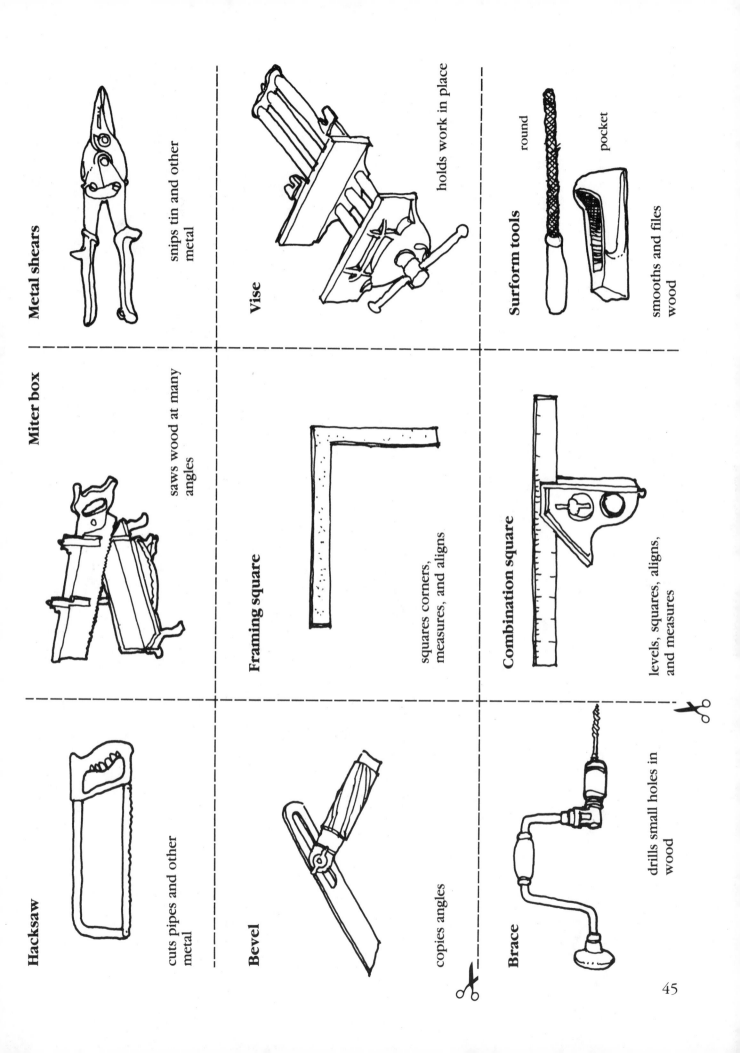

Metal shears

snips tin and other metal

Vise

holds work in place

Surform tools

round

pocket

smooths and files wood

Miter box

saws wood at many angles

Framing square

squares corners, measures, and aligns

Combination square

levels, squares, aligns, and measures

Hacksaw

cuts pipes and other metal

Bevel

copies angles

Brace

drills small holes in wood

45

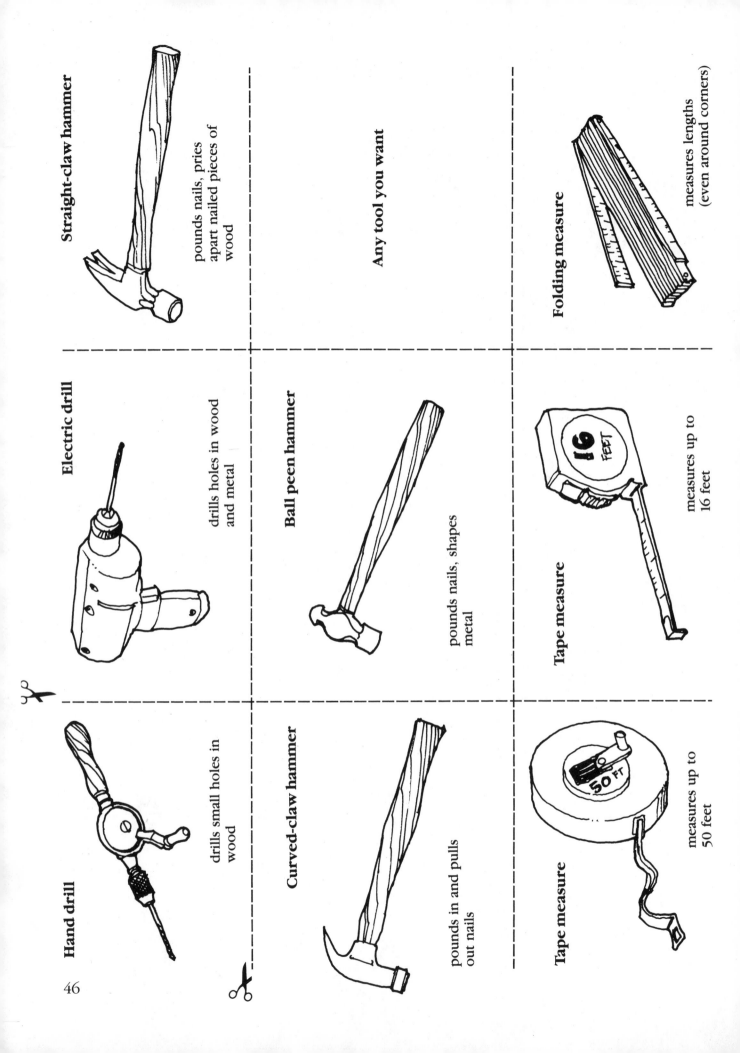

Straight-claw hammer

pounds nails, pries apart nailed pieces of wood

Any tool you want

Folding measure

measures lengths (even around corners)

Electric drill

drills holes in wood and metal

Ball peen hammer

pounds nails, shapes metal

Tape measure

measures up to 16 feet

Hand drill

drills small holes in wood

Curved-claw hammer

pounds in and pulls out nails

Tape measure

measures up to 50 feet

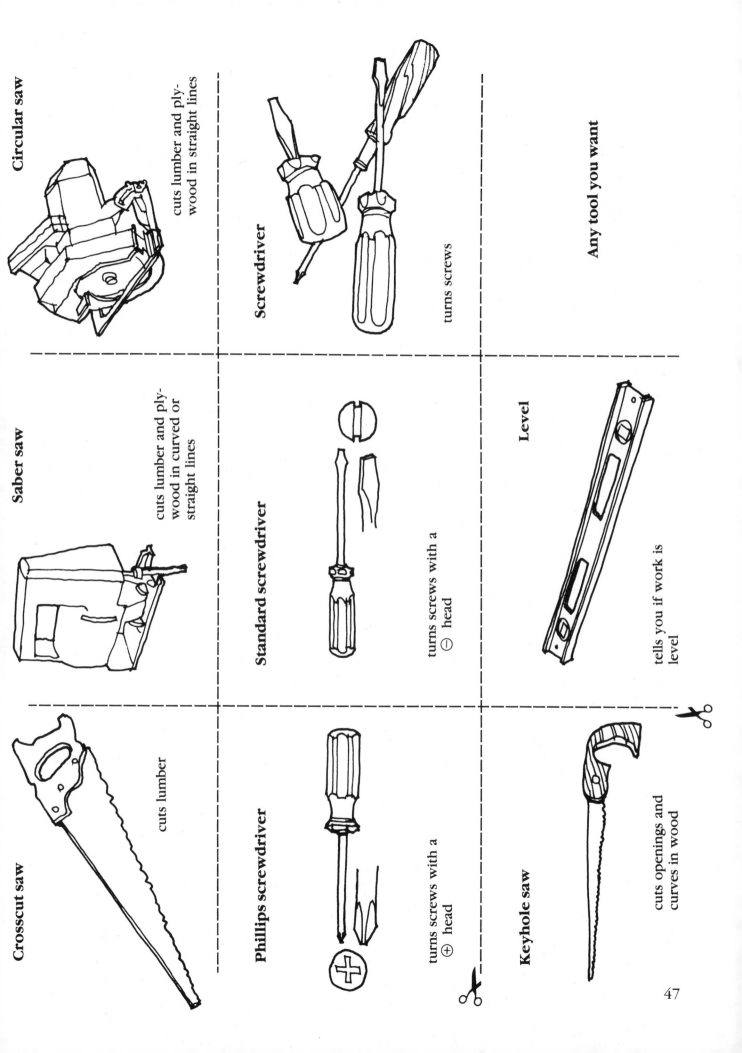

Circular saw

cuts lumber and ply-wood in straight lines

Saber saw

cuts lumber and ply-wood in curved or straight lines

Crosscut saw

cuts lumber

Screwdriver

turns screws

Standard screwdriver

turns screws with a ⊖ head

Phillips screwdriver

turns screws with a ⊕ head

Any tool you want

Level

tells you if work is level

Keyhole saw

cuts openings and curves in wood

47

Tool Vocabulary

Skills
- *Using research sources such as dictionaries, encyclopedias, and catalogs*
- *Developing tool vocabulary*

Time
- *1–2 class periods*

Participants
- *Groups of 2–4 students*

Materials
- *1 copy of each worksheet for each student*
- *Resources such as tool catalogs and repair manuals*

Students investigate functions of tools commonly used in construction trades, electrical work, and electronics. Real experience with tools can help develop spatial reasoning as well as practical skills.

Directions:

Working in groups, the students are given worksheets and directed to use tool catalogs, dictionaries, encyclopedias, or any other resource materials available to find out how each tool is used.

Allow a limited amount of time depending on class ability and interest. Each worksheet should take about 30 minutes.

When all groups have completed most of the sheet, call the class together for discussion. Some possible questions:
- Were any tools hard to find out about? What additional resources would be helpful?
- Are some of the tools used in more than one occupation?
- Which tools seem useful to most people?
- Which occupations need the most tools?
- Do some of the words have more than one meaning?

Note: Since there are no "correct" answers, no answer key is provided. Students should be encouraged to call a store that sells tools for further information.

Extensions:

1) Have students contact people working in occupations that use these tools to find out information on the tools not listed in their reference books.

2) There are three vocabulary lists attached. One or two may be used for homework, with students directed to discuss the tools with members of the family or other adults.

3) Make a list of tools used in each of the following occupations:

Carpenter	Plumber	Sheet metal worker
Cabinetmaker	Electrician	Mover
Surveyor	Laborer	Drafter
Machinist	Meteorologist	Flight engineer

TOOL VOCABULARY

Directions: Use a dictionary, encyclopedia, catalogs, or any other reference source available. For each tool listed, find out what it is used for and who uses it, if possible.

Tool	What Is It Used For?	Who Uses It?
1. Hammer		
2. Chisel		
3. Pliers		
4. Meter stick		
5. Tape measure		
6. Pipe wrench		
7. Plumb line		
8. Lever		
9. Screwdriver (flatblade)		
10. Tsquare		
11. Saw		
12. Drill		
13. Tin snips		
14. Pulley		
15. Level		
16. Clamp		
17. Vise		
18. Straightedge		
19. Jackhammer		
20. Jack		

PROFESSIONAL TOOL VOCABULARY

Directions: Use a dictionary, encyclopedia, catalogs, or any other reference source available. For each tool listed, find out what it is used for and who uses it, if possible.

Tool	What Is It Used For?	Who Uses It?
1. Phillips head screwdriver		
2. Allen wrench		
3. Center punch		
4. Crimping tool		
5. Ball peen hammer		
6. Feeler gauge		
7. Offset screwdriver		
8. Socket wrench		
9. Open-end wrench		
10. Long nose pliers		
11. Slide caliper		
12. Ratchet screwdriver		
13. Rat tail file		
14. Hacksaw		
15. Reamer		
16. Chuck handle		
17. Vise grip pliers		
18. Surform		
19. Miter box		
20. Micrometer		

ELECTRIC AND ELECTRONIC TOOL VOCABULARY

Directions: Use a dictionary, encyclopedia, catalogs, or any other reference source available. For each tool listed, find out what it is used for and who uses it, if possible.

Tool	What Is It Used For?	Who Uses It?
1. Wire stripper		
2. Alignment tool		
3. Burnisher		
4. Soldering iron		
5. Hex-key set		
6. Nutdriver set		
7. Penlight		
8. Crescent wrench		
9. Clip leads		
10. Slip joint pliers		
11. Snap ring pliers		
12. Needle nose pliers		
13. Oblique cutter pliers		
14. Spline key set		
15. Reverse action tweezers		
16. VOM test meter		
17. Lamp extractor		
18. Oscilloscope		
19. Fuse puller		
20. Wire cutter		

Toolin' Around

1234567890123456789012345678901234567890123456789012345678901234567890123456789012345678901234567890123456789012345678901234567890

Skills
- *Learning names and uses of tools*

Time
- *30 minutes*

Participants
- *Groups of 2 students*

Materials
- Toolin' Around *Story Sheet for each student*
- *"Tools" sheet*

Many girls do not have opportunities to learn tool names and uses. This activity provides a review of tools used by workers in construction and other related trades.

Directions:

Distribute a copy of the "Tools" page to each student. Encourage the students to discuss the tools pictured. Which tools are familiar to them? Which are new?

Distribute copies of the Story Sheet. Have the students work together to figure out which tool will do each job.

Review responses with the whole class. Is there always a single "correct" answer?

Extensions:

1) Use this activity in conjunction with *Sort-A-Tool* and *Tool Vocabulary*. See the extensions mentioned for these activities.

2) Have the students choose an occupation mentioned in the story and research the tools that are used in that occupation.

3) Have the students write their own "Toolin' Around" story. Possible sites for such stories might be:
- Construction of a bridge
- Construction of a satellite
- Construction of a solar house

TOOLS

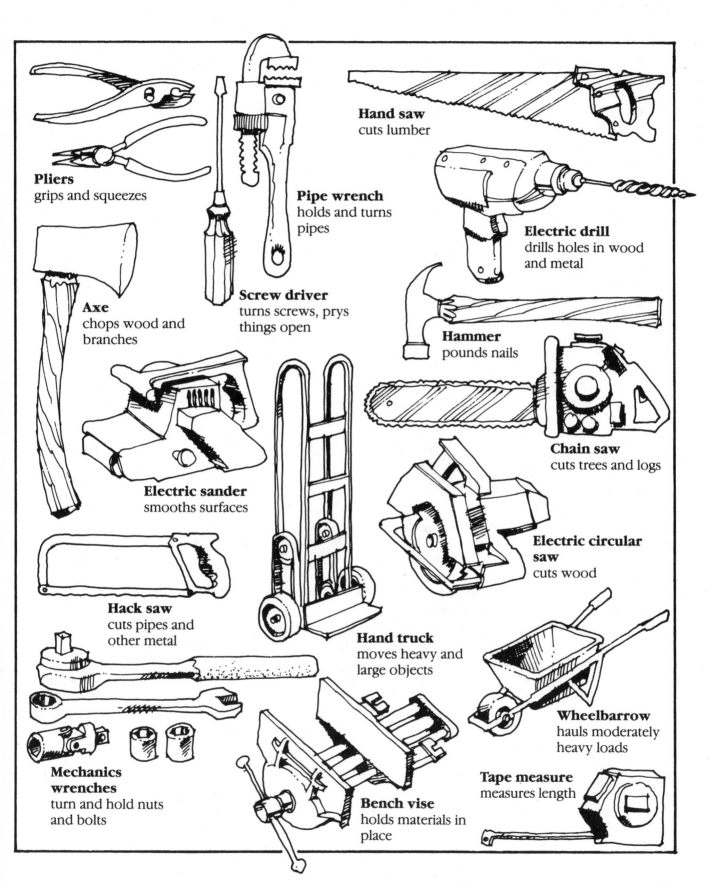

Pliers
grips and squeezes

Pipe wrench
holds and turns
pipes

Hand saw
cuts lumber

Electric drill
drills holes in wood
and metal

Axe
chops wood and
branches

Screw driver
turns screws, prys
things open

Hammer
pounds nails

Chain saw
cuts trees and logs

Electric sander
smooths surfaces

**Electric circular
saw**
cuts wood

Hack saw
cuts pipes and
other metal

Hand truck
moves heavy and
large objects

Wheelbarrow
hauls moderately
heavy loads

**Mechanics
wrenches**
turn and hold nuts
and bolts

Bench vise
holds materials in
place

Tape measure
measures length

53

TOOLIN' AROUND Story Sheet

1234567890123456789012345678901234567890123456789012345678901234567890123456789012345678901234567890123456789012345678901234567890

Directions:
Choose an appropriate tool for each job from those shown on the attached page. Write the names of the tools in the blanks.

Ginny and Joe went with their Aunt Rose to the construction site of a new shopping center. Aunt Rose is a supervisor for the general contractor who is building the shopping center. She was very much interested in building as a child, studied math all through school, took courses in drafting and architecture in college, and later went to work in the building trades. She wanted Ginny and Joe to learn about her work.

The first site they visited will be a pet shop when it is finished. The plumber was working on the piping for the fish tanks. She was holding one pipe in place with a large _____ _____ while using another one to tighten a fitting. She had to cut a pipe to a certain length to fit under the fish tank, so she used a _____ _____ to measure it, then cut it with a _____ _____.

Next, in what would be a clothing store, frames for displays were being built by carpenters. They were using _____ to pound nails into boards they had cut with their electric _____ _____.

As soon as the carpenters had finished, an electrician drilled holes in the frame with her electric _____ so that the wiring for the display lights could pass through the frame. Her partner used screws and a _____ to fasten the switch boxes into place when the wiring was completed. The wires had to be squeezed together with a pair of _____ before being capped off to make them safe.

Two shops away, cabinet makers were sanding cabinets with electric _____ to make the surfaces smooth for painting. They had set up a workbench with a bench_____ on it to hold small pieces of wood they needed to cut to a particular length. Once, when all the electric saws were being used, the cabinet maker used a _____ _____ to cut a wooden brace, holding it in the vise while he cut it.

Out in the mall area, a forklift, which was being used to haul tools and lumber, had stopped running. A mechanic was working on it, with his _____ spread about him on the floor. Several workers could not wait for the forklift to deliver what they needed, so they used a _____ to carry their supplies.

A large appliance store was almost finished, and a refrigerator was being brought in on a hand _____ by a worker who liked to balance the load just right. He almost ran into Ginny because he couldn't see around the big refrigerator.

Joe and Ginny were getting hungry, so Aunt Rose offered them lunch at a nearby hamburger stand. On the way out of the shopping center, Joe noticed that a tree had been blown down nearby, perhaps during a recent windstorm. Workers were using _____ _____ to cut up the large trunk into small pieces. Others were using _____ to chop off some of the very small limbs.

After lunch, Aunt Rose took Ginny and Joe home. Their mother was busy rewiring the electric plug for the toaster, and she suggested that Ginny and Joe apply their knowledge immediately by using the lawn mower to cut the grass!

Spaces Construction Company

1234567890123456789012345678901234567890123456789012345678901234567890123456789012345678901234567890123456789012345678901234567890

Skills
- *Recognizing tools*
- *Visualizing construction jobs*
- *Finding tools to do each task*
- *Using tools in a variety of ways*

Time
- *1 class period*

Participants
- *Groups of 2–4 students*

Materials
- *For each group:*
  Set of tool cards
  Set of Spaces Construction Company *job orders*

In this activity, students decide which tools will help them do small construction jobs. *Sort-A-Tool* and *Tool Vocabulary* should precede this activity so students become familiar with the *tool cards* and some uses of each tool. If possible, bring in actual tools, especially ones new to students.

Directions:

Divide students into groups of 2–4. Give each group a set of *tool cards* and *Spaces Construction Company* job orders. Explain that this is not competitive and they may help each other, just as people do at work.

Place the *tool cards* and the job orders in separate piles face down on the table.

Draw five *tool cards* and lay them *face up* in the center of the table. If an "Any tool you want" card turns up, replace it, and put it back into the stack.

To start the game, each player in turn draws a *Spaces Construction Company* job order and places it face up in her playing space. This is the job she has been assigned. She will need to gather tools to do this job.

To gather tools, each player in turn draws a *tool card* and sets it face up next to her job order. Players help each other decide which part (or parts) of the job can be done with each tool. If the tool is not necessary for that job, the player can *exchange* it for any one of the five *tool cards* face up in the center of the table or *save* it for future use. At the end of each turn then, the player has one more *tool card* and there are still five cards in the center.

Taking turns, players continue to collect *tool cards* and discuss their uses in completing the job. In most cases, there is more than one tool that will do each part of the job, and players may think of ingenious ways to use the tools. Some tasks may be done without tools.

If an "Any tool you want" card is used in completing a job, the desired tool must be named. For example, "This is a hammer" makes that card a hammer for the rest of the game.

When a player has a set of tools that will complete a job order, she must describe the way the tools can be used to do the job. She may then draw a new job order from the stack.

Tools used for one job order may be used again on later jobs. The game ends when all the tasks have been completed.

Extensions:

1) Do an actual construction or repair project. See the References section for suggestions.

2) Have students think of a repair or small construction project they would like to do. What tools and materials are needed? List the steps.

3) Have the students make flowcharts of the construction jobs described on the job orders.

4) Find books in the library about tools and make individual or group reports. Some topics that might be of interest and value:
- Tool safety
- Proper uses of tools
- History of tools
- Manufacture of tools
- Hand tools compared with machine tools
- Care of tools
- Tools for other jobs such as auto repair, metal work, artistry and crafts
- Tools in other cultures

References: *(References are listed in order, from simple to complex.)*

Women's Studies Program. *The House that Jill and Jack Built.* 1976. Berkeley Unified School District, Berkeley, CA.

Boy Scouts of America. *Home Repairs.* Merit Badge series. 1974. North Brunswick, NJ.

Basic Home Repairs Illustrated. 1972. Lane Magazine and Book Co., Menlo Park, CA.

Green, Floyd and Susan E. Meyer. *A Step-by-Step Guide to Major Interior Improvements: You Can Renovate Your Own Home.* 1978. Doubleday & Co., Inc.

Handyman: Complete Guide to Home Maintenance. 1975. Banner Press, New York, NY.

SPACES CONSTRUCTION COMPANY   Job Order No. ___230___

Department: _Carpentry_   **Date:**_____

Description of job: _Make a playhouse with 4 sides and a roof for visiting cousins._

Materials already on job: _3 sheets of plywood, 8 hinges, and screws_

Task:	**Tools used for each task:**
Find the center of each piece of plywood.	
Cut 2 pieces of plywood in half for 4 walls.	
Drill holes to start cuts for window and door.	
Cut 1 window and 1 door.	
Smooth all edges.	
Attach hinges by screws to connect 4 walls.	
Set roof on top. Hold for inspection.	

- ✂

SPACES CONSTRUCTION COMPANY   Job Order No. ___231___

Department: _Sheet metal_   **Date:**_____

Description of job: _Install rain gutters on front of house._

Materials already on job: _Lengths of metal gutter, metal stripping, ladder, nails_

Task:	**Tools used for each task:**
Measure lengths of gutter.	
Cut gutter to length.	
Wrap metal stripping around the gutter.	
Nail gutter to edge of roof.	
Check to see if the rain water will go down.	

SPACES CONSTRUCTION COMPANY   Job Order No. __232__

Department: _Picture framing_   **Date:**_____

Description of job: _Prepare frame for new picture._

Materials already on job: _Lengths of antique oak, wood glue_

Task:

Measure the picture to find frame size.

Measure the oak for the sides of the frame.

Cut 45° angles at the corners.

Glue the corners.

Attach sides together with screws or small nails.

Hold corners together tightly until glue dries.

Tools used for each task:

SPACES CONSTRUCTION COMPANY   Job Order No. __233__

Department: _Woodshop_   **Date:**_____

Description of job: _Build window box for marigold and daisy plants._

Materials already on job: _Lumber, nails_

Task:

Measure wood for sides and bottom of box.

Cut boards to length.

Drill holes in bottom for drainage.

Nail sides and bottom of box together.

Level the window box.

Nail box to outside of house, under window.

Tools used for each task:

Name:

SPACES CONSTRUCTION COMPANY   Job Order No. __234__

Department: ___Carpentry_____   Date: _____

Description of job: ___Build dog house with 4 sides and a tin roof._____

Materials already on job: _____Lumber, 1 sheet of tin, nails_____

Task:

Measure lumber. _____

Cut wood for sides. _____

Cut door opening. _____

Nail sides together. _____

Measure tin roofing. _____

Cut tin roofing. _____

Nail roof in place. _____

Tools used for each task:

_____

_____

_____

_____

_____

_____

_____

- -

Name:

SPACES CONSTRUCTION COMPANY   Job Order No. __235__

Department: ___Woodshop_____   Date: _____

Description of job: ___Build wooden bookcases for new book store._____

Materials already on job: _____Lumber, wood screws_____

Task:

Measure height of books and plan shelf spaces. ___

Measure lumber. _____

Cut wood for frame and shelves. _____

Make sure the shelves are level. _____

Drill starter holes for the screws. ___

Assemble bookcase with wood screws. ___

Tools used for each task:

_____

_____

_____

_____

_____

_____

59

Name: _____

SPACES CONSTRUCTION COMPANY   Job Order No. __236__

Department: _Hardwood woodshop_ _____ **Date:** _____

Description of job: _Make a wooden skateboard._ _____

Materials already on job: _Large piece of paper, hardwood, set of wheels, screws_ _____

Task:

Trace the shape of the skateboard you want. _____

Cut wood to fit the pattern. _____

Smooth the wood and round corners. _____

Drill holes for screws. _____

Attach the wheels with screws. _____

_____

_____

Tools used for each task:

_____

_____

_____

_____

_____

_____

_____

- -

Name: _____

SPACES CONSTRUCTION COMPANY   Job Order No. __237__

Department: _Outdoor carpentry_ _____ **Date:** _____

Description of job: _Make a bike rack to hold 10 bikes._ _____

Materials already on job: _Lumber for rack frame, dowels* for uprights, nails_ _____

Task:

Measure the lumber and the dowels. _____

Cut dowels and boards to correct lengths. _____

Drill holes for dowels. _____

Nail frame together. _____

_____

_____

_____

Tools used for each task:

_____

_____

_____

_____

_____

_____

_____

*Dowels are cylinders of wood. These dowels are 1" in diameter and 3' long.

60

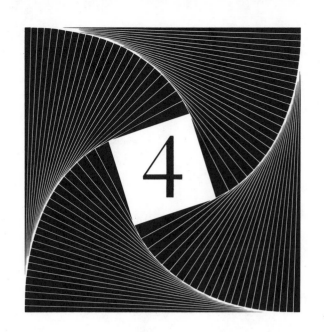

ATTITUDES AND PERSONAL GOALS

Cooperative Logic Problems

1234567890123456789012345678901234567890123456789012345678901234567890123456789012345678901234567890123456789012345678901234567890

Skills
- *Logical reasoning*
- *Organizing data*
- *Cooperating*
- *Using models*
- *Checking*

Time
- *1–2 class periods*

Participants
- *Groups of 4–6 students*

Materials
- *Copies of problem sheets, prepared according to directions below.*

These logic problems encourage students to work cooperatively. Each student has a clue important to the solution. Some of the problems use manipulative pieces that can be moved to check solutions.

Preparation:

Make one copy of each problem for each group of 4–6 students. Cut each sheet into the 6 separate clue pieces. Save any additional parts, such as the vegetables and the garden plot. (An envelope makes good storage space for each problem and its parts.)

Directions:

Explain to the students that they will be working on logic problems. One way to introduce the idea of logic problems is to draw the analogy with detective stories. First you meet the characters involved and find out the problem. Typically, you want to discover who committed a crime. As the story progresses and clues are presented, the list of suspects is narrowed until only one remains and the mystery is solved. This process of elimination based on clues is similar to the reasoning used by doctors and mechanics when diagnosing medical or mechanical ailments.

Each problem is to be solved cooperatively. Students need to work together to find an answer. Emphasize that each person will have different clues, so it is important to listen as each clue is read.

Give each student within the group one clue to the logic problem. If there are more than four students in a group, use the extra pieces that are starred (*). All problems can be solved with the four unstarred clues. Clues given on the starred pieces may be helpful, but are not necessary for solving the problem. Students may read their clues to each other but *may not show each other the written clues.*

Hands-on Logic

The first four problems have movable parts which can be organized and reorganized by anyone in the group to try out possible solutions. The statement of the problem is on all clue cards in these first four problems. You may want to discuss the content or wording of some of the logic problems before doing them, such as:

• **Garden:** The orientation is important. For example, "to the right of" means toward the right side of the garden as you face the plot, and "next to" means adjacent to the crop named.

• **Planets:** This will be an interesting problem for students who do not yet know the order of the planets. The actual distances of the planets from the sun vary as each planet travels its orbit. Numerical values for the distances are not needed to determine the order of the planets out from the sun.

Other Logic Problems

The last four cooperative logic problems have the problem statement on just one of the clue cards. Remind students to listen for the problem statement.

Students may want to make grids to keep track of the clues on some of the problems. For example, for *Who Has Which Job?* this grid might be useful:

	lawyer	electrician	doctor
Lois			
John			
Melina			

Extensions:

1) Have students make up their own cooperative logic problems.

2) Additional logic problems can be found in:

• Harnedek, Anita. *Deductive Thinking Skills,* (Mind Benders). 1978. Midwest Publications, Box 129, Troy, MI 48099.

• Summers, George. *Test Your Logic.* 1972. Dover Publications, Inc., 180 Varick St., New York, NY 10014.

• Williams, Wayne. *Quizzles.* 1976. Dale Seymour Publications, P.O. Box 10888, Palo Alto, CA 94303.

The format of this activity was adapted from the *Green Box,* Humboldt County Schools, Office of Environmental Education, Eureka, CA.

BACK

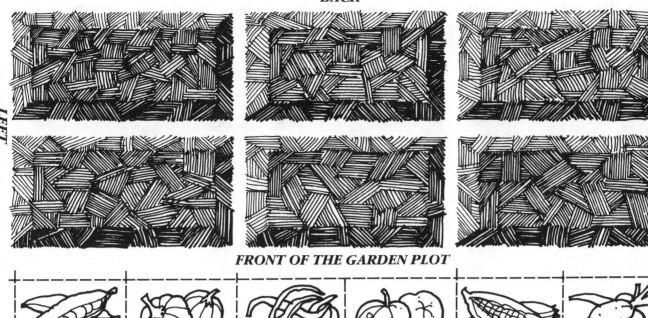

FRONT OF THE GARDEN PLOT

| Peas | Melons | Beans | Tomatoes | Corn | Carrots |

LEFT / **RIGHT**

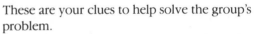

Garden

These are your clues to help solve the group's problem.

Read them to the group, but do not show them to anyone.

Problem: Which crop is planted in each of the sections of the garden?
• The melons are to the right of the beans.

Garden

These are your clues to help solve the group's problem.

Read them to the group, but do not show them to anyone.

Problem: Which crop is planted in each of the sections of the garden?
• The beans are planted in front of the corn.
• The peas are next to the tomatoes.

Garden

These are your clues to help solve the group's problem.

Read them to the group, but do not show them to anyone.

Problem: Which crop is planted in each of the sections of the garden?
• The peas are next to the corn.
• The melons are to the right of the carrots.

Garden

These are your clues to help solve the group's problem.

Read them to the group, but do not show them to anyone.

Problem: Which crop is planted in each of the sections of the garden?
• The tomatoes are in back of the melons.

Garden*

These are your clues to help solve the group's problem.

Read them to the group, but do not show them to anyone.

Problem: Which crop is planted in each of the sections of the garden?
• The carrots are in front of the peas.

Garden*

These are your clues to help solve the group's problem.

Read them to the group, but do not show them to anyone.

Problem: Which crop is planted in each of the sections of the garden?
• The carrots are next to the beans.

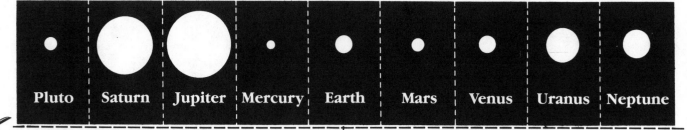

| Pluto | Saturn | Jupiter | Mercury | Earth | Mars | Venus | Uranus | Neptune |

Planets

These are your clues to help solve the group's problem.
Read them to the group, but do not show them to anyone.

Problem: Arrange the nine planets in order based on their relative distance from the sun.

- The five planets nearest the sun are Earth, Jupiter, Mercury, Venus, and Mars, not necessarily in that order.

Planets

These are your clues to help solve the group's problem.
Read them to the group, but do not show them to anyone.

Problem: Arrange the nine planets in order based on their relative distance from the sun.

- Early astronomers knew that Venus and Mercury were the only two planets closer to the sun than our planet Earth.
- Saturn is nearer Earth than Neptune.

Planets

These are your clues to help solve the group's problem.
Read them to the group, but do not show them to anyone.

Problem: Arrange the nine planets in order based on their relative distance from the sun.

- The five planets furthest from the sun are Uranus, Neptune, Jupiter, Pluto, and Saturn, not necessarily in that order.
- Four of the planets are much larger than the other five planets, but have a lower density.

Planets

These are your clues to help solve the group's problem.
Read them to the group, but do not show them to anyone.

Problem: Arrange the nine planets in order based on their relative distance from the sun.

- Mercury and Pluto have seven planets between them.
- There is just one planet between Uranus and Pluto.

Planets*

These are your clues to help solve the group's problem.
Read them to the group, but do not show them to anyone.

Problem: Arrange the nine planets in order based on their relative distance from the sun.

- Uranus is between Saturn and Neptune.
- The five terrestrial or earthlike planets are Earth, Pluto, Venus, Mars, and Mercury.

Planets*

These are your clues to help solve the group's problem.
Read them to the group, but do not show them to anyone.

Problem: Arrange the nine planets in order based on their relative distance from the sun.

- Copernicus in the 16th century knew of six planets: Earth, Mars, Mercury, Jupiter, Saturn, and Venus. These are the six planets closest to the sun.
- Earth is 93 million miles from the sun.

April	Sharon	Gloria
SUN CAR	SOLAR STOVE	PLANT/PEST CHART
3rd prize	2nd prize	1st prize

Ecology Fair

These are your clues to help solve the group's problem.
Read them to the group, but do not show them to anyone.

Problem: Find out who did which project and who won which prize.

- The first prize went to the SUN CAR, a model of a solar powered car.
- Gloria would like to become a biologist.

Ecology Fair

These are your clues to help solve the group's problem.
Read them to the group, but do not show them to anyone.

Problem: Find out who did which project and who won which prize.

- The finalists were April, Sharon, and Gloria, not necessarily in that order.
- The second prize winner made soup on her SOLAR STOVE for all her friends.

Ecology Fair

These are your clues to help solve the group's problem.
Read them to the group, but do not show them to anyone.

Problem: Find out who did which project and who won which prize.

- The following projects won the top three prizes in the Ecology Fair: SOLAR STOVE, PLANT/PEST CHART, and SUN CAR.
- Gloria won third prize.

Ecology Fair

These are your clues to help solve the group's problem.
Read them to the group, but do not show them to anyone.

Problem: Find out who did which project and who won which prize.

- The SOLAR STOVE used reflectors angled to intensify the sun's heat.
- April had never seen a sun-powered car before the Ecology Fair.

Ecology Fair*

These are your clues to help solve the group's problem.
Read them to the group, but do not show them to anyone.

Problem: Find out who did which project and who won which prize.

- All the prize winners in the Ecology Fair were 14 years old.
- April bought a copy of the PLANT/PEST CHART from the third prize winner.

Ecology Fair*

These are your clues to help solve the group's problem.
Read them to the group, but do not show them to anyone.

Problem: Find out who did which project and who won which prize.

- Several years of study and gardening were summarized in the PLANT/PEST CHART, a guide to plants that repel garden pests.
- Sharon enjoyed the soup April made.

Camel	Giant salamander	Gray seal	Human	Killer whale	Tortoise

Animal Ages

These are your clues to help solve the group's problem.

Read them to the group, but do not show them to anyone.

Problem: Find the longest life span for each animal.

- A giant tortoise has been known to live four times as long as a giant salamander.
- The oldest person on record was a woman who lived to be 113 years old.

Animal Ages

These are your clues to help solve the group's problem.

Read them to the group, but do not show them to anyone.

Problem: Find the longest life span for each animal.

- A giant salamander lived twice as long as the oldest camel.
- The oldest person lived 23 years longer than the oldest killer whale.

Animal Ages

These are your clues to help solve the group's problem.

Read them to the group, but do not show them to anyone.

Problem: Find the longest life span for each animal.

- A killer whale lived one year less than the oldest gray seal and giant salamander combined.
- Tortoises are one of the few animals that live longer than people.

Animal Ages

These are your clues to help solve the group's problem.

Read them to the group, but do not show them to anyone.

Problem: Find the longest life span for each animal.

- The oldest gray seal lived to be 41 years old.
- Giant tortoises have the longest life span of all living creatures except bacteria.

Animal Ages*

These are your clues to help solve the group's problem.

Read them to the group, but do not show them to anyone.

Problem: Find the longest life span for each animal.

- The oldest tortoise lived almost five times as long as the oldest gray seal.
- People have been known to live over four times as long as the oldest camel.

Animal Ages*

These are your clues to help solve the group's problem.

Read them to the group, but do not show them to anyone.

Problem: Find the longest life span for each animal.

- The oldest tortoise was over twice as old as the most ancient killer whale.
- Some gray seals live longer than camels.

WHO HAS WHICH JOB

Who Has Which Job?

These are your clues to help solve the group's problem.

Read them to the group, but do not show them to anyone.

- The electrician, lawyer, and doctor in Ellensburg are named Melina, Lois, and John, but not necessarily in that order.
- John is the lawyer's neighbor.

Who Has Which Job?

These are your clues to help solve the group's problem.

Read them to the group, but do not show them to anyone.

Problem: What are the names of the only electrician, lawyer, and doctor in Ellensburg?

- The electrician is John's daughter.
- The doctor and lawyer both have Siamese cats.

Who Has Which Job?

These are your clues to help solve the group's problem.

Read them to the group, but do not show them to anyone.

- Lois and the lawyer have the same birthday but one is 25 years older than the other.
- All three people earn over $20,000 a year.

Who Has Which Job?

These are your clues to help solve the group's problem.

Read them to the group, but do not show them to anyone.

- The doctor treated Lois for a burned hand.
- John, Melina, and Lois all live on Mulberry Street.

Who Has Which Job?*

These are your clues to help solve the group's problem.

Read them to the group, but do not show them to anyone.

- Melina and the electrician swim together often.
- John, Lois, and Melina have known each other for 20 years.

Who Has Which Job?*

These are your clues to help solve the group's problem.

Read them to the group, but do not show them to anyone.

- Melina and John took math together in high school.
- The electrician fixed the wiring in the doctor's house.

Who Will Be Accepted?

These are your clues to help solve the group's problem.

Read them to the group, but do not show them to anyone.

- Lawrence, Amy, Steven, and Betty are competing for entrance into the College of Engineering.
- Amy has taken more math than Steven.

Who Will Be Accepted?

These are your clues to help solve the group's problem.

Read them to the group, but do not show them to anyone.

- Betty has taken more math than Steven.
- The academic math classes at their high school are: Algebra I, Geometry, Algebra II, and Calculus. They must be taken in this order.

Who Will Be Accepted?

These are your clues to help solve the group's problem.

Read them to the group, but do not show them to anyone.

- These four students are equally qualified except for the number of math courses taken. Each has taken at least one academic math class.
- Lawrence has taken more math than Betty.

Who Will Be Accepted?

These are your clues to help solve the group's problem.

Read them to the group, but do not show them to anyone.

Problem: Find the most advanced math course taken by each student. Who will be accepted into the College of Engineering?

- Lawrence has taken one year less math than Amy.
- One of these students will be accepted to the College of Engineering.

Who Will Be Accepted? *

These are your clues to help solve the group's problem.

Read them to the group, but do not show them to anyone.

- Lawrence enjoyed Geometry the most of all his math classes.
- Steven did not take Geometry.

Who Will Be Accepted? *

These are your clues to help solve the group's problem.

Read them to the group, but do not show them to anyone.

- Amy has taken more math than Betty.
- Steven wishes he had taken more math in high school.

Salary Scramble

These are your clues to help solve the group's problem.
Read them to the group, but do not show them to anyone.

- A computer systems operator earns $3,130 more than a secretary.
- A school teacher averages $17,447 a year.

Salary Scramble

These are your clues to help solve the group's problem.
Read them to the group, but do not show them to anyone.

- A computer systems operator averages $43,670 less than a pilot.
- A teacher averages $4,297 less than a carpenter.

Salary Scramble

These are your clues to help solve the group's problem.
Read them to the group, but do not show them to anyone.

- A teacher earns almost as much as a computer systems operator, only $883 a year less.
- An engineer averages $10,086 a year more than a carpenter.

Salary Scramble

These are your clues to help solve the group's problem.
Read them to the group, but do not show them to anyone.

Problem: What is the average yearly salary of each profession?

- An engineer earns $30,170 less than a pilot.
- A secretary earns $2,247 less than a teacher.

Salary Scramble*

These are your clues to help solve the group's problem.
Read them to the group, but do not show them to anyone.

- A pilot earns more than 3 times as much as a teacher.
- There is a difference of $46,800 between the highest and lowest salary.

Salary Scramble*

These are your clues to help solve the group's problem.
Read them to the group, but do not show them to anyone.

- The salaries of the pilot and the secretary together total $77,200.
- An engineer earns over twice as much as a secretary.

Favorite Class

These are your clues to help solve the group's problem.

Read them to the group, but do not show them to anyone.

- Calculus, physics, auto mechanics, and music are some of the classes offered at Hilldale High.
- The auto mechanics class is working on an old Chevy engine.
- Calculus is only available to seniors.

Favorite Class

These are your clues to help solve the group's problem.

Read them to the group, but do not show them to anyone.

Problem: Find the favorite class of Paul, Rose, Don, and Emily.

- One girl dropped physics because she was the only girl in class.
- Paul is unhappy in Don's favorite class.
- No two students have the same favorite class.

Favorite Class

These are your clues to help solve the group's problem.

Read them to the group, but do not show them to anyone.

- In Emily's favorite class she is regrinding valves.
- Each student is currently enrolled in his/her favorite class.
- Paul, who thought he would enjoy a class in music, hates it.

Favorite Class

These are your clues to help solve the group's problem.

Read them to the group, but do not show them to anyone.

- Paul and Don are juniors.
- Rose is a senior and hopes to major in electrical engineering in college.
- Each student's favorite class is one of those mentioned in these clues.

Favorite Class*

These are your clues to help solve the group's problem.

Read them to the group, but do not show them to anyone.

- Paul is enrolled in three of the four classes mentioned.
- Rose is glad she took physics her junior year because of the conflict with calculus this year.
- Paul has curly red hair.

Favorite Class*

These are your clues to help solve the group's problem.

Read them to the group, but do not show them to anyone.

- Emily wants to enter an apprenticeship program when she graduates from school.
- Both calculus and physics are offered 5th period only.
- Don refuses to take any science because it might ruin his grade point average.

GARDEN

PLANETS

The planets in order from the sun are:

        Mercury
        Venus
        Earth
        Mars
        Jupiter
        Saturn
        Uranus
        Neptune
        Pluto

ECOLOGY FAIR

1st prize	2nd prize	3rd prize
Sharon	April	Gloria
Sun Car	Solar Stove	Plant/Pest Chart

ANIMAL AGES

Giant tortoise	200 years
Human	113 years
Killer Whale	90 years
Giant salamander	50 years
Gray seal	41 years
Camel	25 years

WHO HAS WHICH JOB?

Melina	Lawyer
Lois	Electrician
John	Doctor

WHO WILL BE ACCEPTED?

Amy	Calculus
Lawrence	Algebra II
Betty	Geometry
Steven	Algebra I

Amy will be accepted.

SALARY SCRAMBLE[1]

The teacher's salary is the reference point.

Pilot	$62,000
Engineer	31,830
Carpenter	21,744
Computer Systems Operator	18,330
Teacher	17,447
Secretary	15,200

FAVORITE CLASS

Emily	Auto mechanics
Rose	Calculus
Don	Music
Paul	Physics

1. These are average salaries. Figures are based on data from 1981 Bureau of Labor Statistics publications. A comprehensive discussion of these and other occupations (including salary information) can be found in the most recent *Occupational Outlook Handbook* available from U.S. Dept. of Labor, Bureau of Labor Statistics, 450 Golden Gate Ave., Box 36017, San Francisco, CA 94102.

Typical Day

Skills
- *Writing*
- *Interviewing*
- *Making reports*

Time
- *1–2 class periods plus homework*

Participants
- *Individual*

Materials
- *None*

An exploration of the adult working day is initiated through student descriptions of their impressions of a typical Wednesday in the life of a person in a certain occupation, and then continued by student interviews of the people they have described.

Directions:

Point out that we often have misconceptions about jobs. We tend to glamorize certain jobs such as police detective, model, and flight attendant. Other jobs such as bookkeeper and librarian we tend to think of as dull and repetitious.

Tell the students that they will compare their *impressions* of specific jobs with *real* information provided by workers in those jobs.

Assignment:

Identify an adult who does a specific job. The adult may be a parent or friend. If you have specific career interests, consider someone in the community employed in that occupation.

Write and turn in a paper that you think describes a typical Wednesday (24 hours) in the life of this person.

Make an appointment with and interview this person. Ask specific questions that refer to the description you wrote, such as: What time do you wake up? How do you get to work? What do you do at work? Do you work alone or with others? What time do you leave work? What do you do after dinner?

Ask the adult these additional questions: What preparation did you need for this job? When did you decide to enter this field? What do you like about your job?

Write and turn in a new description of the adult's typical Wednesday.

Discussion:

• Compare the descriptions written before and after the interview.
• What things were similar and what were different?
• Were there any surprises in the interview?
• What kind of skills did the person need for the job he or she was doing?
• What preparation did the person need for the job?
• Why did the person choose his or her particular field?

Evaluation:

Have the students evaluate the activity. Was it useful? Was it interesting? Are there other things they would like to know now? Do they want to try it again for a new person with a different job?

Extensions:

1) Students can give oral reports to the class on their interviews.

2) Have the students make circle graphs of the adult worker's typical day.

3) Have the students practice interviewing each other before interviewing a working adult.

I'll Probably Be . . .

Skills
- *Organizing data*
- *Graphing*
- *Presenting data*

Time
- *1 class period*

Participants
- *Groups of 2 or 3 students*

Materials
- *Unlined paper*
- *Rulers*

Students practice organizing information and making graphs based on their own career choices.

Directions:

Ask the students to think about what job or career they would like to have as an adult. Ask them to write the occupation on a slip of paper. Collect the slips and list all the jobs on the chalkboard.

Divide the class into groups of two or three. Each group's task is to make a visual graph of the information on the board. They can organize the information in any way they like and make any type of graph (line, bar, circle, etc.).

When the students have completed the assignment, collect the graphs and display them around the room. Discuss the graphs. What were the various ways of organizing the information? Are some easier to read than others? Are some easier to understand than others?

Extensions:

When the students write the occupation on a slip of paper, have them indicate whether they are male or female. Have the groups of students make two graphs: one for the boys' choices and one for the girls' choices. Are there any differences in career choices? If so, in what fields and why?

Building a Schedule of Classes

1234567890123456789012345678901234567890123456789012345678901234567890123456789012345678901234567890123456789012345678901234567890

The first time a young person encounters a school scheduling process is an excellent opportunity to develop a number of skills. Tell your students to imagine they are 7th graders about to select their class schedules for the first time. While it is exciting to be able to choose their courses, it also can be confusing or frustrating.

This activity will help students understand how to organize information, set priorities, and make decisions.

Directions:

Give each pair of students two copies of each worksheet and one copy of the Course Schedule Chart. Review the Chart and, if necessary, work out the first schedule on the chalkboard with the class.

The given schedule is based on a representative junior high school course schedule. It is limited to offerings for 7th grade students. This permits both simplicity and variety in course offerings. The exercises give practice in:

• making a schedule from a given set of available periods
• revising a schedule under both voluntary and involuntary situations
• correcting an erroneous schedule
• developing a schedule, given required courses

No answers are provided since answers will vary in most cases. Students may compare their results to check each other.

Skills
• *Organizing information*
• *Interpreting charts*
• *Using elimination process for making decisions*

Time
• *1–2 class periods*

Participants
• *Individual or groups of 2 students*

Materials
• *1 copy of each of the two worksheets for each student (The worksheets may be used together or separately.)*
• *1 Course Schedule Chart for each pair of students*
• *Pencils and erasers*

Extensions:

A similar exercise can be made from your own school's course offerings.

COURSE SCHEDULE CHART　　　7th Grade

Eugene Junior High, Eugene, Oregon

TEACHER	PERIOD 1	PERIOD 2	PERIOD 3	(Lunch) PERIOD 4	(Lunch) PERIOD 5	PERIOD 6	PERIOD 7
Rapp	Lang. Arts	SS/Am. West	SS/Am. West			SS/Am. West	Lang. Arts
Banks	SS/Colonial America		SS/Colonial America	SS/Am. West	SS/Colonial America		EJH Publishing
Page	**		Lang. Arts	**		Lang. Arts	Lang. Arts
Hamm	Children's Theatre	Shakespeare Act. Comp.			Lang. Arts	**	**
Rice	Spanish I	**	**		Spanish I	**	
Eymann		Adv. Reading	Read/rite	Read/rite		Adv. Reading	**
Keyes	**		Typing	Typing	Typing	Typing	
Figueroa	**	**	Math 7		Math 7		**
Uno	**	**	Arithmetic	**			**
Square	Adv. Math 7		**	Adv. Math 7		Math 7	**
Van Metre		Math 7		Math 7	Math 7	**	**
O'Ryan	Space Science		Space Science		**	**	Space Science
Baer	Lang. Arts	SS/Colonial America			Forestry Science	Forestry Science	Forestry Science
Ravel	Needlecraft		Needlecraft	Action Wear	Action Wear		Survival Clothing
Chow	Home Cooking	Home Cooking			You Are What You Eat	You Are What You Eat	Survival Foods
LaPlume	Drawing	Cartooning	Art & Design		Drawing		Sculpture
Tiffany	Painting/Printmaking	Painting/Printmaking	Stained Glass	— at Gomez Elementary School —			
Potter	**			Ceramics	Ceramics	Graphics/Lettering	Graphics/Lettering
Hammar	Wood Survey	Toymaking	Toymaking		Sm Engine Mechanics	Wood Survey	
Barr	Music Survey	Beg. Band		Int. Band	Adv. Band	Music Survey	
Octavio		**	Orchestra		Guitar	Choir	Guitar
Akido		Physical Education	**	Physical Education		**	**

**Teachers with non-7th grade courses or supervision duties*

BUILDING A SCHEDULE OF CLASSES — Worksheet I

1) Agnes wants to enroll in the following courses. The class periods for which they are offered are listed to the right. Note that she must take Small Engine Mechanics during 5th period because that is the only time it is offered. When can she have her lunch period? Circle each selected period. Cross off the 4th and 5th periods listed for other courses and then select class periods for her other courses. She will need something for periods 1 through 7.

CLASS PERIODS

	1	2	3	4	5	6	7
Math 7		•		•	•	•	
Space Science	•		•				•
Language Arts	•		•			•	•
SS: Colonial America	•	•	•		•		
Physical Education		•		•			
Small Engine Mechanics					⊙		
Lunch					•	•	

2) Alonzo's courses are listed below. Finish his schedule in two different ways.

CLASS PERIODS

	1	2	3	4	5	6	7
Math 7						•	
Beginning Band		•					
Language Arts	•		•			•	•
Lunch					•		
SS: Colonial America	•		•				
Physical Education					•		
Space Science	•		•				•

CLASS PERIODS

	1	2	3	4	5	6	7
Math 7						•	
Beginning Band		•					
Language Arts	•		•			•	•
Lunch				•			
SS: Colonial America	•		•				
Physical Education				•			
Space Science	•		•				•

3) Andrea selected the following schedule. When she enrolled in the courses she found that her Painting/Printmaking course 2nd period was "closed" because too many students had enrolled already. Revise her schedule to allow her to take Painting/Printmaking during 1st period.

CLASS PERIODS

	1	2	3	4	5	6	7
Advanced Math 7	⊙			•			
Language Arts	•		•			•	⊙
SS: American West			•	⊙	•	•	
Physical Education			•		⊙		
Painting/Printmaking	•	⊙					
Lunch					•	⊙	
Forestry Science					•	⊙	•

CLASS PERIODS

	1	2	3	4	5	6	7
Advanced Math 7	•			•			
Language Arts	•		•			•	•
SS: American West			•	•	•	•	
Physical Education			•				
Painting/Printmaking	•	•					
Lunch					•	•	
Forestry Science					•	•	•

4) Alan chose this schedule. His best friend, Annabelle, has Social Studies (American West) during 3rd period. Rearrange his schedule to have Social Studies with her.

CLASS PERIODS

	1	2	3	4	5	6	7
Math 7			•		•	⊙	•
Language Arts		•	⊙			•	•
SS: American West			•	•	•	⊙	
Space Science		•		•			⊙
Physical Education			⊙		•		
Lunch				⊙	•		
Wood Survey	⊙					•	

CLASS PERIODS

	1	2	3	4	5	6	7
Math 7		•		•	•	•	
Language Arts	•		•			•	•
SS: American West		•	•	•		•	
Space Science	•		•				•
Physical Education				•			
Lunch					•	•	
Wood Survey	•					•	

BUILDING A SCHEDULE OF CLASSES   Worksheet II

1234567890123456789012345678901234567890123456789012345678901234567890123456789012345678901234567890123456789012345678901234567890

Use the 7th grade Course Schedule Chart to help these students.

1) Alfredo has chosen these courses. Write when each course is offered and find a schedule for him.

CLASS PERIODS

	1	2	3	4	5	6	7
Language Arts							
SS: American West							
Physical Education							
Advanced Math 7							
Forestry Science							
Cartooning							
Lunch							

2) Andy made this schedule but it contains errors. Find the errors and make a correct schedule for him.

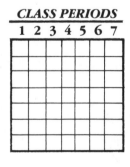

CLASS PERIODS

	1	2	3	4	5	6	7
Language Arts							
SS: Colonial America							
Math 7							
Forestry Science							
Music Survey							
Lunch							
Physical Education							

3) Adrienne wishes to take Language Arts, SS: Colonial America, Advanced Math 7, Forestry Science, Physical Education, and Toymaking. Make a class schedule for her.

CLASS PERIODS

	1	2	3	4	5	6	7
_____							
_____							
_____							
_____							
_____							
_____							
_____							

4) Ali is your best friend. He is on vacation and must take Math 7, Language Arts, SS: American West, and Physical Education. He needs a science course and one elective (other course of any kind). Select these courses for him and prepare his schedule.

CLASS PERIODS

	1	2	3	4	5	6	7
_____							
_____							
_____							
_____							
_____							
_____							
_____							

5) Pretend you are attending this junior high. Select courses and prepare a schedule for yourself.

CLASS PERIODS

	1	2	3	4	5	6	7
_____							
_____							
_____							
_____							
_____							
_____							

Fear of Math: Fact or Fantasy?

1234567890123456789012345678901234567890123456789012345678901234567890123456789012345678901234567890123456789012345678901234567890

Collecting, analyzing, and displaying data are vital skills for scientific and technical occupations. This activity allows the student researcher to develop these skills within the classroom.

Directions:

Discuss with the class the fear of math and whether there is a difference in how boys and girls feel about math. What could be some of the reasons for these differences? Decide with the class to research this topic among the boys and girls at your school.

Develop a Math Skill Survey (see sample included):

• Divide the class into groups of 3.
• Have each group brainstorm questions that might appear on a comprehensive math exam.
• Go around the room and have each group suggest a possible question for the survey.
• Continue until each group has contributed 2 or 3 questions.
• Decide with the class which 10 questions will appear on your survey.
• Work out the answer key.

Develop a Math Attitude Questionnaire (see sample included):

Have the students brainstorm multiple choice questions that will pinpoint attitudes such as:
• initial feelings about test
• how their parents would feel when they found out about the special test
• whether they were worried about passing the test
• how they feel about math in general

Go around the room and have each group suggest possible questions about math attitudes.
Put the questions on the chalkboard.
Each group of 3 will analyze one question. Decide on the 10

Skills
• *Organizing*
• *Graphing*
• *Predicting*
• *Displaying information*

Time
• *2–3 class periods*

Participants
• *Groups of 3 students*

Materials
• *Math Skill Survey and Math Attitude Questionnaire, both developed by class*
• *Paper on which to display graphs*

best questions and which group will be responsible for which question.

Include space for student age and sex on the questionnaire.

Plan for Survey:

Decide with the class what group of students you will research, and how you will do it; for example: other math classes, all 9th grade math classes, or entire school during second period.

Obtain permission to conduct the survey from the administration and other teachers or classes involved in your research project.

Pilot Survey:

Have the class do the sample survey and questionnaire as a pilot activity. Analyze the questions for sex differences and make minor revisions before giving the survey and questionnaire to your research group.

Administer Skill Survey and Attitude Questionnaire:

Distribute copies of the Skill Survey and allow the students to begin working. After 5 minutes, collect the papers and administer the Attitude Questionnaire.

Tally and Graph Information:

Have the students decide how to tally the information.

Let each group decide how they will display their conclusions and information in graph form.

Reports to Class:

Have each group give a report to the class on what they found and how their graph displays this information.

Display Project:

Place the entire student research project in the school library, main office, or gymnasium, where the rest of the school population can see the results.

Have a student summarize and write an article for the school paper.

This idea originated with Robbie Roberts, 7th grade student, Sinaloa Junior High, Novato, California, and was submitted as his entry in the 1980 Math/Science Fair. He won the 7th grade math division. Following is a modified version of his math survey and student questionnaire.

MATH SKILL SURVEY   (Sample)

The following problems are representative of math problems that students of your grade level can solve. You will not have time to finish all the problems. If you do not know how to do a problem, go on to the next one.

GROUP A

_____ **1)** ROUND OFF 20.658 to the nearest whole number.

_____ **2)** ADD: 714; 877; 1301.

_____ **3)** FIND THE AREA of this rectangle.

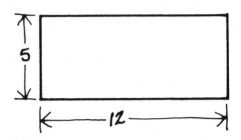

GROUP B

_____ **1)** ADD: $5\frac{3}{4}$; $3\frac{5}{8}$; $4\frac{1}{2}$.

_____ **2)** WRITE 925% as a decimal number.

_____ **3)** SOLVE for the value of X: $2X - 20 = 18$.

GROUP C

_____ **1)** DIVIDE: $\frac{7}{8}$ by $\frac{1}{6}$

_____ **2)** FIND THE VALUE OF X: $5X + 7 = 3X - 39$.

_____ **3)** WHAT NUMBER is 20% less than 5?

GROUP D

_____ **1)** If an 8-inch pizza serves two, how many should two 12-inch pizzas serve?

_____ **2)** If the length and width of a rectangle are each increased by 25%, by what percent is the area increased?

_____ **3)** If Sandy scored 14 baskets out of 20 shots in a basketball game, what is her percentage of accuracy?

MATH ATTITUDE QUESTIONNAIRE   (Sample)

You have just seen a page of math problems. Without thinking about the answers to these problems, please answer the following questions. Don't spend much time in deciding your answer. There is no grade for this section of your math exercise. This is an effort to find out what effect a math test has on your feelings. *Put the letter of the most correct answer in the space.*

_____ **1)** When handed this math survey, my immediate feeling was
    (a) This is important. I'll do the best that I can.
    (b) I'm not going to take this test seriously.
    (c) I wish I had stayed home today.

_____ **2)** I wondered how my parents would feel when they found out that I had a special test. They might be
    (a) very concerned.
    (b) a little concerned.
    (c) not at all concerned.

_____ **3)** If I thought I might not pass the test I would
    (a) be very worried.
    (b) be a little worried.
    (c) not be worried at all.

_____ **4)** I thought that the test would be used
    (a) to place me in next fall's math class.
    (b) for grading me in this class.
    (c) for nothing.

_____ **5)** If I thought I wouldn't do well on this test I
    (a) would try to do the best that I could.
    (b) wouldn't try very hard.
    (c) would try to find a way to get out of it.

_____ **6)** My folks
    (a) insist I get good grades in math.
    (b) encourage me to get good grades in math so I can be anything I want.
    (c) don't care what grades I get in math.

_____ **7)** If another student in class always scored higher than I did on math tests, I would like to
    (a) score higher than this student on the test.
    (b) beat the student but realize I probably wouldn't.
    (c) not really care whether I beat the student or not.

_____ **8)** On this math survey
    (a) the girls would probably do better than the boys.
    (b) the boys would probably do better than the girls.
    (c) there wouldn't be any difference between boys and girls in our class.

_____ **9)** When I think about going into a math or science field, I
    (a) think of all the possibilities there are in math and science.
    (b) don't think I'll be good enough to consider a career in math or science.
    (c) am not interested in going into a math or science field.

_____ **10)** I think that math tests are
    (a) a challenge.
    (b) scary.
    (c) boring.

My age _____ **My sex** _____

This is Your Lifeline

Skills
- *Graphing*
- *Metric measuring*
- *Sequencing*
- *Decision making*
- *Planning*
- *Estimating*

Time
- *1 class period*

Participants
- *Individual*

Materials
- *1 copy of Student Instructions for each student*
- *Strips of adding machine tape 30 cm long, 1 for each student*
- *Crayons or marking pens: the same 2 colors should be available for each student. For example, education may be marked in red and employment may be marked in blue. All students should use the same colors in order to create the graphic effect. Sharing of crayons or pens will help.*
- *Scotch tape*
- *Metric rulers*

Each student is asked to make a plan for his or her life and to graph it on a time line. This process can increase a student's awareness of the relationship between education and employment options.

Directions:

Tell the students that they are going to imagine what will happen to them during their lives. Ask them to take a minute to list several things they think might occur.

When they have made their individual lists, put a few of the items on the chalkboard to help other students think of things they might have missed.

Give each student a strip of tape, along with the sheet of instructions. (See Student Instructions.) Give the students 15 minutes to complete their own lifelines.

As the lifelines are completed, have the students tape them into position on the chalkboard. The graph may be more significant if lifelines for girls are put together in one column and boys in another column.

The most important part of this activity is the open-ended discussion. Some of the students will have made unrealistic life plans. The discussion ties in the relationship between high school courses and employment options.

Discussion:

Question: Which is greater, the time spent in education or in working? (Read from graph.)

Question: How does education time compare with time after retirement? (Read from graph.)

Question: Did many people choose to stay home with small children? (Read from graph.)

Question: How long did most people work? (Read from graph.)

Question: Was there a difference in the graphs for boys and girls? Who worked longer? Who attended more school? Who retired earlier?

Fact: On an average, an American man works 45 years and retires at age 65. About one-half of his life is spent in the workforce.

Fact: On an average, a married American woman works 25 years outside the home. The average unmarried woman works 43 years. Considering a woman's life expectancy today, this is at least one-third of her life. There is a rapid increase in the number of women working each year and a trend toward working more years.

Question: What education is necessary for the career choices on the students' lifelines?

Fact: A student planning his or her life might keep in mind the definite relationship between jobs that pay higher salaries and jobs that require a math background. Math skills allow maximum flexibility and opportunity in this technological world.

Fact: Math courses are sequential. Important decisions regarding high school courses are made in junior high school. To complete the precalculus sequence in most high schools, a student must acquire the basic skills in 7th and 8th grades, take Algebra I in 9th, Geometry in 10th, Algebra II in 11th, and Math Analysis and Trigonometry in 12th.

Fact: Calculus is considered elementary mathematics. We need to recognize it as a starting place, not an ending place. Without high school preparation, many students will eliminate themselves from the majority of college majors.

Question: Which careers probably bring the highest salaries?

Fact: Many fields that previously required no math are becoming technologically oriented. Technology is used in such diverse occupations as food processing, milking cows, and running libraries. Advancement opportunities often depend on math and science backgrounds. Students will open many options by taking as much math and science as possible in high school.

84

THIS IS YOUR LIFELINE

Student Instructions

You should have a strip of paper 30 cm long for your lifeline.

You should also have made a list of the things you think will happen to you during your life.

Directions:

1) On one end, write whether you are a male or female.

2) Write the year you were born on the same end.

3) Assume that you will live 100 years. Along one edge of the paper, make a mark for each 10-year period. (Let 3 cm represent 10 years.)

4) Mark the year you started school.

5) Mark the year you plan to finish school. Do you plan to finish high school? College? Get an advanced degree?

6) Mark the year you plan to first begin working full-time.

7) Mark the year you plan to retire from work or stop working. Are there times in your life when you stop working and then begin again after a few years? Mark those times.

8) Color all the Education Years with the color your teacher tells you.

9) Color all the Employment Years with the color your teacher tells you.

10) Fill in any other important dates on your lifeline.

11) Write in other information: What kind of job do you have? Do you marry? Do you have children?

12) Tape your lifeline onto the class graph.

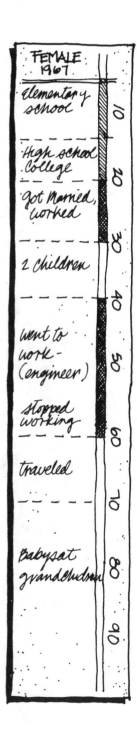

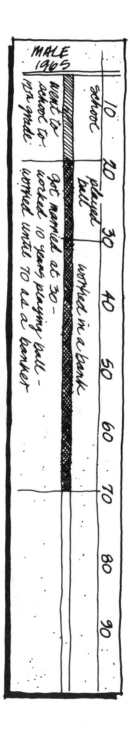

Math: What's It All About?

1234567890123456789012345678901234567890123456789012345678901234567890123456789012345678901234567890123456789012345678901234567890

Using a questionnaire that looks at their own feelings and ideas about mathematics, the students develop an awareness of the need for good math skills.

Directions:

Inform the students that they will be exploring the nature and need for mathematics. There are no right or wrong answers. The intent of this activity is to expand the students' awareness of what mathematics is, why we study it, and the importance of good math skills in today's job market. Students should try to answer each question.

Hand out copies of the Student Questionnaire sheet and allow students 5–10 minutes to answer questions.

After the students have completed the questionnaire, discuss the questions with the class. Encourage many responses to each question.

Extensions:

Have the students develop a math questionnaire for parents. The students would then poll the adults they know on how they use mathematics in their lives.

MATH: WHAT'S IT ALL ABOUT?   Student Questionnaire

1) What I like best in math is _____

_____

_____

2) I know you need good math skills if you want to be a(n) _____

_____

_____

3) Arithmetic includes adding, subtracting, multiplying and dividing of whole numbers, fractions, and decimals. Other math topics I have studied are _____

_____

_____

4) The math courses I intend to take in high school are _____

_____

_____

5) Math and other sciences belong together because _____

_____

_____

6) The science courses I intend to take in high school are _____

_____

_____

7) When I finish school I hope to _____

_____

_____

8) I find math difficult to understand when it comes to _____

_____

_____

9) I have used math outside of school to _____

_____

_____

10) The reason we study mathematics in school is _____

_____

_____

Viewpoints

1234567890123456789012345678901234567890123456789012345678901234567890123456789012345678901234567890123456789012345678901234567890

Skills
- *Understanding different points of view*

Time
- *1–2 class periods*

Participants
- *Groups of 4 students*

Materials
- *1 copy of a situation for each group. (Some groups may have the same situation depending on the number of students you have.)*

This is a discussion activity to help students think about the factors and controversies involved in career choices. The situation descriptions can be used as discussion starters or may be role-played. Either form should be kept nonthreatening and nonjudgmental, since the intent is to understand opposing points of view. There are no "right" or "wrong" solutions.

Directions:

Divide the class into groups of 4. Explain to the students that they will be in discussion groups to consider some situations that might arise related to career decisions. Describe the following steps to the class:
- Each group is given a situation. Each student is given one slip that states the situation from one person's point of view.
- The students discuss the situation by representing their part.
- Students may want to ask the other characters for information and opinions. What advice does each character have to offer?
- Students should try to come to a consensus on the problem.

When all the groups have finished, at the end of a designated time, or on the following day, reconvene the class as a whole. One person from each group describes the group's scenario to the class and reports each character position and the resolution the group arrived at.

After each group's report, or at the conclusion of all group reports, introduce the following questions for class discussion:
- Are these situations familiar? Which arguments do you find the most convincing? Why?
- Have you heard some of these arguments in real life?
- Would any of the decisions or opinions be different if the student in the situation was of the other sex?
- Why do you think it's important for boys and girls to be able to enroll in courses or work in careers that are usually considered appropriate for only one sex?
- What are some fields from which women are usually excluded? Men?
- Do you know people working in nontraditional areas?

Extensions:

1) Have students locate in your community a man or a woman working in a nontraditional field and interview that person about his or her work.

2) Have the students discuss (or role-play) the characters from different scenes. For example, have a discussion from the point of view of all of the counselors, or a discussion including all of the students of the various scenarios.

You are Abbie's parent. Abbie missed 7 days from her Algebra class during the first month of school because of a trip with the school choir. You agree with Abbie that she should drop Algebra.

You don't like all the pressure she has been under trying to catch up in Algebra. Ever since the choir trip she's been studying 2 or 3 hours a night, but it doesn't seem to help. She says she missed so much it's hard to understand the new ideas. She dreads going to Algebra class now. If she starts disliking math she'll never take enough math to go into engineering. You feel it's best if she drops Algebra now and takes it next semester.

Abbie's counselor invited you to this meeting with Abbie and her Algebra teacher.

SITUATION A   Abbie

You are Abbie. You missed 7 days of your Algebra class during the first month of school because of a trip with the school choir. You're having a hard time making up all the work and want to drop out of Algebra and start again next semester. You're beginning to hate math because you have to work so hard, and because you missed so much that it's hard to understand the new ideas in class. If you stay in Algebra you're afraid you'll get a bad grade.

You want to be an engineer and your math grades will be important. However, if you do drop the class you may not be able to finish all the math classes you need in high school. If necessary, you'd be willing to take additional math during the summer to complete all the math requirements for engineering.

You have requested to drop Algebra. Your counselor has called a meeting with you, your parent, and your teacher.

You are Abbie's counselor. Abbie has requested to drop Algebra after missing 7 days of class during the first month of school because of a trip with the school choir. You feel Abbie needs to work harder to catch up and finish the course. If she does drop Algebra now, it will be too late in the semester for her to join an academic class. This would mean her pre-college program will fall behind schedule. Abbie wants to be an engineer, so she needs to take 4 years of math in high school.

You have called this meeting with Abbie, her parent, and her teacher to discuss the situation.

--→

SITUATION A   Abbie's Teacher

You are Abbie's teacher. Abbie missed 7 days of class during the first month of school because of a trip with the school choir. She is having a hard time making up all of the class work she missed, and she wants to drop out of Algebra class and start again next semester.

You feel Abbie should work harder and finish the course even if she doesn't get a good grade. You think Abbie can catch up. If she drops Algebra now, she won't be able to finish all of the math classes she needs in high school to study engineering.

Abbie is one of the few young women you have had who has expressed any interest in engineering. You want to encourage her in this aspiration, so you hate to see her quit Algebra now.

Abbie's counselor asked you to come to this meeting with Abbie and her parent.

You are Mark. It is time to sign up for next semester's classes at school. There are two Algebra courses offered: a one-year Algebra course and a two-year (somewhat easier) Algebra course. You don't know for sure what you want to major in, but you want to take the one-year course so that by the time you graduate from high school you will have all the math you might need for a full choice of college majors.

Your counselor tells you there is room for only one more student in the one-year course, and it is more important to put another student in that class. The other student is a young woman, Anne, who has a high grade-point average and wants to be a doctor. Since she was quite young, she has planned to go to medical school.

You are at a meeting of your counselor, Anne, and the Algebra teacher to discuss which of you should take the one-year Algebra class next semester.

SITUATION B   Algebra Teacher

There are two Algebra courses offered at your school: a one-year Algebra course and a two-year (somewhat easier) Algebra course. You are scheduled to teach the one-year Algebra course for next semester. The counselor has informed you there is room for only one more student in the one-year Algebra class. Two students, Mark, and a young woman, Anne, want to take the one-year course. Mark plans to go to college but has not chosen a major; the young woman has a high grade-point average and has planned, since she was quite young, to go to medical school.

You really don't care which student is placed in the class but are determined to keep the class size at its limit which is 30 students. Last year, another counselor talked you into taking just "one" more student and before you knew it there were 41 students in the class. You feel it is important to keep your class size at the negotiated contract level, 30 students.

The counselor has called a meeting of Mark, Anne, and you to discuss the situation.

You are Anne. It is time to sign up for next semester's classes at school. There are two Algebra courses offered: a one-year Algebra course and a two-year (somewhat easier) Algebra course. You have a high grade-point average and plan to be a doctor. You need to take the one-year Algebra course so you can take all the math required to be a pre-med student in college. You have planned to go to medical school since you were quite young.

There is only one spot left in the one-year Algebra class and another student, Mark, also wants to take it. He wants to take 4 years of math in high school so he can have a full choice of majors in college.

His counselor has called a meeting with you, the Algebra teacher, and Mark to discuss the situation.

---→

You are Mark's counselor. It's sign-up time for next semester's classes at school. At your high school there are two Algebra classes offered: a one-year course and a two-year (somewhat easier) course. There is room for only one more student in the one-year Algebra class. Both Mark and a young woman, Anne, who plans to be a doctor, want to take the one-year course. Mark plans to go to college but has not chosen a major; the young woman has a high grade-point average and has planned, since she was quite young, to go to medical school.

You feel Anne should take the one remaining spot in the one-year Algebra course and Mark should take the two-year course, or wait to take the one-year Algebra later.

You have called a meeting of Mark, Anne, and the Algebra teacher to discuss the situation.

You are Barbara's mother. Barbara is in her junior year at high school. Last semester her school offered an Explore The Trades course for the first time. She took the course and found she was interested in welding. She would like to take the regular welding class her senior year and possibly enter an apprenticeship program after high school.

This is disturbing to you. You don't know anything about welding and feel it's an unsuitable field for a woman.

You married young, raised Barbara and her two brothers and, in addition, worked part-time as a secretary when the family needed money. You hope Barbara won't have to work at all when she gets married. If she does have to work, you don't want it to be in welding.

Barbara's counselor has arranged a meeting with you, Barbara, and Barbara's father to discuss Barbara's future plans.

SITUATION C — Barbara

You are Barbara. You are in your junior year of high school. Last semester a course called Explore The Trades was offered at your school for the first time. Since you like working with your hands, you decided to take the course and found you really enjoyed it, especially the welding part. You would like to take the regular welding course next year and possibly enter an apprenticeship program after high school.

Your parents seemed disturbed by your interest in welding. They want you to marry and raise a family without having to work. If you do have to work, they feel welding is unsuitable for a woman.

Your counselor has arranged a meeting with you and your parents to discuss your future plans.

93

You are Barbara's father. Barbara is in her junior year at high school. Last semester her school offered an Explore The Trades course for the first time. She took the course and found she was interested in welding. She would like to take the regular welding class her senior year and possibly enter an apprenticeship program after high school.

This is disturbing you. You hope Barbara will marry and raise a family without having to work. If she does have to work, she should choose to be a secretary or something easy to do part-time. A career in welding would be very demanding and would interfere with raising a family. Besides, welding is dangerous and you do not want your daughter doing a man's job.

Barbara's counselor has arranged a meeting with you, Barbara, and Barbara's mother to discuss Barbara's future plans.

SITUATION C   **Barbara's Counselor**

You are Barbara's counselor. Barbara is in her junior year of high school. Last semester her school offered an Explore The Trades course for the first time. She took the course and found she was interested in welding. She would like to take the regular welding class her senior year and possibly enter an apprenticeship program after high school. You are pleased that Barbara would like to learn more about welding. The reason the Explore The Trades course was offered was to expose students, especially girls, to the job opportunities available in the trades.

Barbara's parents seem disturbed by her interest in welding. They want her to marry and raise a family without having to work. If she does have to work, they feel a career in welding is unsuitable.

You have arranged a meeting with Barbara and her parents to discuss Barbara's future plans.

5

JOB REQUIREMENTS AND DESCRIPTIONS

Career Cards

Guessing at job definitions gives students information about the work involved in a number of careers.

Skills
- *Increasing career awareness*

Time
- *1 class period*

Participants
- *Individual*

Materials
- *Set of career definition slips (1 slip per student) A or B*
- *Set of answer record sheets (1 slip per student)*
- *Scotch tape*
- *Pencils*

Preparation:

Duplicate and cut apart career definition slips A or B and answer sheets. If desired, career slips may be glued or taped to 3″ × 5″ cards. In a class of 30, several students will have the same question.

Note: Set A refers to scientific or technical careers. Set B includes career titles from the trades. Either set or both may be used, depending on class make-up and interest. If both sets are used, allow extra discussion time.

Directions:

Ask the students to list on paper all the jobs they can think of.

Call on students to suggest jobs to list on the chalkboard. If possible, categorize the jobs (science, business, professions, trades, etc.). Avoid general terms such as "worker" or "scientist"; ask the students to decide what kind of worker or scientist. Keep the list on the chalkboard until the activity is over.

Discuss briefly what each job means. Be sure the jobs for the activity are on the list, and that students understand their definitions.

Demonstrate the activity with four students in front of the class. Tape a sample job slip on one student's back (see pages 97 and 98 for sample slips), and provide an answer sheet and pencil. Have that student ask each of the other three students to read *silently* the job description, then state an answer. Explain that answers may differ or be the same. It may be necessary to demonstrate with two different questions.

When all students understand the process, tape a sign on each student's back and give each student an answer sheet. Students get up and walk around gathering answers from other students. When they have three answers, they sit down, take off the card and look at it, keep the card and answer list, and wait until all students have finished.

When all students are seated, ask the students who have question number 1 to stand. Call on each student in turn to read the question and read the three answers received. List the answers on the chalkboard. Give the correct answer. Look at the other answers. Are they equally correct? If not, why?

Continue until each student has given his or her answers and all occupations have been discussed.

Discuss the game and the reasons for putting the cards on the students' backs. Did it make the activity more interesting? Did the students like getting up and moving around to give answers rather than sitting at their seats and raising their hands? Were some students glad they were reporting the answers of others and, therefore, not responsible for the answer?

Extensions:

Have students make up their own list of jobs and definitions.

Answer Key:

A. Sciences Careers	*B. Trades Careers*
1. Marine biologist	**1.** Carpenter
2. Engineer	**2.** Locksmith
3. Accountant	**3.** Computer operator
4. Geologist	**4.** Plumber
5. Astronomer	**5.** Cement mason
6. Meteorologist	**6.** Draftsperson
7. Botanist	**7.** Forester
8. Architect	**8.** Electrician
9. Chemist	**9.** Sheet metal worker
10. Veterinarian	**10.** Welder
11. Doctor	**11.** Bricklayer
12. Archeologist	**12.** Baker

Sample Items

1. A person who cleans teeth in a dentist's office is called a _____.

Dental hygienist

2. A person who develops programs for computers is a _____.

Computer programmer

1) A scientist who studies fish and other ocean life is called a _____.   **A**

7) A person who studies plant life is called a _____.   **A**

2) A person who makes practical use of the sciences to design and build bridges is called an _____.   **A**

8) A person who designs buildings is called an _____.   **A**

3) A person who works all day with numbers is called an _____.   **A**

9) A scientist who works with chemicals to learn about the properties of materials is a _____.   **A**

4) A scientist who studies the rock and minerals of the earth is a _____.   **A**

10) A person who tells owners how to take care of sick animals is called a _____.   **A**

5) A person who makes observations of the stars and the universe can be called an _____.   **A**

11) A person who finishes medical school is called a _____.   **A**

6) A scientist who studies the atmosphere to understand and predict the weather is a _____.   **A**

12) A person who studies ancient ruins is called an _____.   **A**

1) A person who builds or repairs wooden structures is called a

_____ . **B**

7) A person who plans and supervises planting and cutting of trees is called a _____ . **B**

2) A person who makes keys is called a _____ . **B**

8) A person who installs and repairs electrical equipment and electrical wiring is called an

_____ . **B**

3) A person who runs programs on a computer is called a

_____ . **B**

9) A person who makes metal ducts for air-conditioners or furnaces is called a

_____ . **B**

4) A person who works on the pipes and fixtures of the water systems of houses is called a

_____ . **B**

10) A person who joins metal together by fusing or heating is called a _____ . **B**

5) A person who mixes, pours, and finishes concrete is called a

_____ . **B**

11) A person who would build a fireplace is called a

_____ . **B**

6) A person who makes drawings for engineers and scientists is called a_____ . **B**

12) A person who makes many loaves of bread every day is called a_____ . **B**

Who Am I?

Skills
- *Using tens and hundreds*
- *Recognizing spatial transformations*
- *Solving story problems*
- *Coordinate graphing*
- *Identifying geometry vocabulary*
- *Completing function tables*
- *Applying number logic*

Time
- *1–2 class periods*

Participants
- *Individual*

Materials
- *Copy of each worksheet for each student. (Some worksheets may be omitted, if desired.)*

Solving letter codes through a series of problem-solving math activities, students gain information about some careers.

Directions:

Read about each person's occupation. Learn what the career is by solving the problems and matching the letters to your solutions.

Extensions:

1) Worksheets may be used for homework if students already have the skills involved.

2) The activities may be used to introduce a skill or to provide review or checkup. Some of these pages may cover skills not usually included in the curriculum for your grade level. You may omit those sheets, but consider letting your students try to solve the problems with a little instruction.

Answers:

Tens and Hundreds . . . . MECHANIC

Spatial Transformations . . . . VETERINARIAN

Story Problems . . . . FOREST RANGER

Coordinate Graphing . . . . SURVEYOR

Geometry Vocabulary . . . . SCHOOL TEACHER

Functions . . . . HOTEL CHEF

Number Logic . . . . CARPENTER

WHO AM I?   Tens and Hundreds

1234567890123456789012345678901234567890123456789012345678901234567890123456789012345678901234567890123456789012345678901234567890123456789012345678901234567890

Linda has always loved cars. She has always liked helping take care of the family's car. She checks the oil, checks the tire air pressure, and adds water to the radiator. She is always careful to do a good job whenever she helps and sometimes she is better than her older sister at fitting the parts together.

To find Linda's job, put the right code letter in each blank.

Code Letters

10 more than 100 is . . . . _____ **A**

4 times 10 is . . . . _____ **C**

100 less than 500 is . . . . _____ **E**

10 less than 60 is . . . . _____ **H**

100 more than 1300 is . . . . _____ **I**

10 times 200 is . . . . _____ **M**

1200 divided by 10 is . . . . _____ **N**

_____   _____   _____   _____   _____   _____   _____   _____

2000   **400**   **40**   **50**   **110**   **120**   **1400**   **40**

WHO AM I?

Spatial Transformations

1234567890123456789012345678901234567890123456789012345678901234567890123456789012345678901234567890123456789012345678901234567890

Laurie has always loved animals. She takes care of all of her family's pets and knows what to do when they get sick or injured. She is planning to take a lot of science and math. She wants to go to a special school to prepare for her profession.

To find Laurie's job, put the right code letter over each "transformation" picture below.

CODE LETTERS

A

E

I

N

R

T

V

WHO AM I?   Story Problems

Larry wanted a job that was active and would let him stay outdoors most of the time. He likes learning about animals and plants in school. He wants to travel, and doesn't mind staying by himself. He and his family have always done a lot of camping.

To find Larry's occupation, put the right code letter in each blank below.

Write your answers here:	Code Letters	
_____	A	12 pairs of shoes with one shoe missing, how many shoes left?
_____	E	43 marbles, 5 fell out of my pocket. How many marbles in my pocket?
_____	F	2 elephants, 6 turkeys. How many feet?
_____	G	Three different numbers added together equal 6. What is the biggest number?
_____	N	13 + 45 + 32. Take 10 from each number and add the rest.
_____	O	3 trips to and from the store, 6 blocks away. How many blocks in all?
_____	R	4 points + 5 points + 15 points.
_____	S	10 − 2 + 65 − 3 + 0 − 20
_____	T	26 test questions. 4 wrong. How many right?

___ ___ ___ ___ ___ ___   ___ ___ ___ ___ ___ ___

20   36   24   38   50   22   24   23   60   3   38   24

WHO AM I?   Coordinate Graphing

Luke would rather work outdoors. He is interested in how the land is shaped and notices little things like whether the sidewalk is level or crooked. He likes to travel and would like to help plan big projects such as bridges and dams.

To find Luke's job, put the code letter that matches each number pair in the right blank.

The first letter of each number pair tells how far across, and the second number tells how far up. For example, the letter "x" is at (7,1).

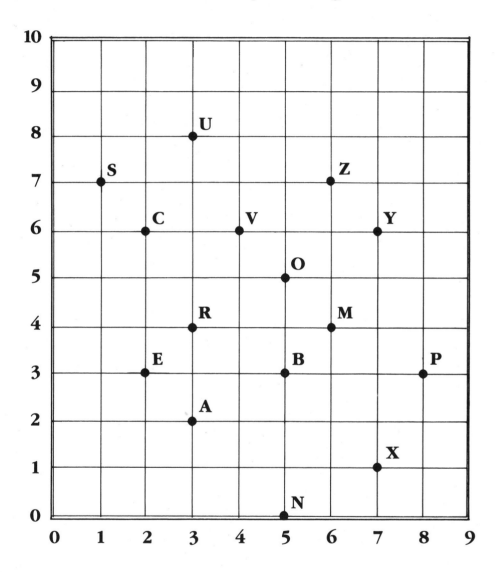

_____   _____   _____   _____   _____   _____   _____   _____

(1,7)   (3,8)   (3,4)   (4,6)   (2,3)   (7,6)   (5,5)   (3,4)

Leo has always enjoyed taking care of the younger children in his family. He has always been good at thinking of games for them to play, and he always knew how to keep them so busy they didn't have time to fight. He likes math, reading, and science, and he knew what courses he had to take to get into college.

To find Leo's occupation, put the code letter over each shape that matches the word.

Code Letters

A	diagonal of a rectangle
C	right angle
E	diameter
H	radius
L	trapezoid
O	parallel lines
R	pentagon
S	ray
T	line segment

WHO AM I?   Functions

Lonnie liked to eat so much that his father helped him learn to cook. He enjoys making up new recipes and trying them out. Sometimes his parents let him plan and cook a whole dinner. He is always careful to plan enough for all the people who come.

Each of these is a function machine. When a number is put into the machine, it follows its own rule and a certain number comes out.

To learn what Lonnie's job is, find the pattern for each function table, and write in the missing number. Put the matching code letter in the blank below.

IN	OUT
2	5
6	9
4	7
3	___
	(C)

IN	OUT
15	20
30	35
20	25
___	10
	(E)

IN	OUT
2	0
5	3
9	7
13	___
	(F)

IN	OUT
2	4
6	12
13	26
10	___
	(H)

IN	OUT
2	10
5	25
7	35
6	___
	(L)

IN	OUT
136	3
459	5
322	2
104	0
276	___
	(O)

IN	OUT
12	3
42	6
15	6
10	1
11	___
	(T)

___ ___ ___ ___ ___   ___ ___ ___ ___

20   **7**   **2**   **5**   **30**   **6**   **20**   **5**   **11**

WHO AM I?

Louise likes building things. When she was only five years old she built a birdhouse, with her mother's help. She can use a saw and a hammer, and she knows how to measure and plan ahead so she won't waste wood. Some day she wants to build a house.

In each row, a shape is always the same number. The same shape may stand for a different number in another row.

To find out what Louise's job is, put the right code letter in each blank.

Code Letter

$$\hexagon + \hexagon + \hexagon = 9 \qquad \hexagon = \underline{} \quad \textbf{A}$$

$$\bigcirc - \square = 3 \text{ and } \bigcirc + \square = 13 \qquad \bigcirc = \underline{} \quad \textbf{C}$$

$$\hexagon + 1 = \triangle \text{ and } \triangle + \hexagon = 5 \qquad \hexagon = \underline{} \quad \textbf{E}$$

$$\diamond - 1 = \square \text{ and } \square + 3 = 7 \qquad \diamond = \underline{} \quad \textbf{N}$$

$$\triangle + 1 = \cap \text{ and } \cap + 6 = 7 \qquad \triangle = \underline{} \quad \textbf{P}$$

$$\square + \triangle = 7 \text{ and } \square + \square = 8 \qquad \square = \underline{} \quad \textbf{R}$$

$$\square \times \bigcirc = \square \qquad \bigcirc = \underline{} \quad \textbf{T}$$

8	3	4	0	2	5	1	2	4
—	—	—	—	—	—	—	—	—

What's My Line?

Skills
- *Estimating*
- *Pattern finding*
- *Logical reasoning*
- *Computing percent*

Time
- *1 class period*

Participants
- *Individual*

Materials
- *Copy of each worksheet for each student*

Students gain information about careers by solving codes keyed to mathematical problems.

Directions:

Read about each woman's occupation. Learn what the career is by solving the problems and matching the letters to your solutions.

Extensions:

1) Have students pick an occupation and make up their own "What's My Line" sheets.

2) Put the problems on cards or smaller pieces of paper and have students work in a group to solve the problem cooperatively. (See Cooperative Logic.)

3) Divide the class into teams and use the sheets for a math relay in which each student does one problem and passes the sheet to the next student. The last person fills in the blanks at the bottom of the page.

Answers:

- Rita Alcala is a Computer Programmer.
- Judy Gold is a Park Ranger.
- Katherine Donahue is a Certified Public Accountant.
- Louise Scott is a Navy Jet Pilot.

107

WHAT'S MY LINE?　　　　　　　　　　　　　Estimation

Rita Alcala has just entered a relatively new and exciting career field with a great opportunity for advancement. Having always been interested in secret codes and complicated languages, she finds herself as good at communicating with machines as she is with other people. In preparing for her career, Rita was glad she took as many high school math courses as possible since it made her college experience easier and more rewarding. In this career, a person must have good reasoning ability and patience to work with very small details. All of Rita's work is performed indoors with modern machinery and a pleasant atmosphere that is dust free and has a moderate temperature. Her job is divided equally between meeting the needs of people who want certain information and understanding the capabilities of complex machines.

Learn what Rita's career is by matching the letters and your solutions below.

Estimate to the nearest whole number the answer to each exercise.

A: $7.9 + 12.6 + 1.3$　　　　　　**M:** 2.05×14.5

I: $2.93 \times 5.16 \times 2.99$　　　　**U:** $.9 + 15.6 + 23 + .007$

O: $26.11 - 2.9$　　　　　　　　**T:** $50 - 15.912$

G: $15.7 + .9 + 2.98$　　　　　　**R:** $.49 \times 23.9$

C: $28.4 - .97$　　　　　　　　**P:** $19.86 - 4.9$

D: $17.7 \div 5.7$　　　　　　　　**E:** $49.2 \div 4.9$

___ ___ ___ ___ ___ ___ ___ ___
27　23　30　15　40　34　10　12

___ ___ ___ ___ ___ ___ ___ ___ ___ ___
15　12　23　20　12　22　30　30　10　12

WHAT'S MY LINE?

Estimating Percent

Judy Gold's career is ideally suited to her lifestyle. She enjoys working with people, taking care of plants and animals, and being outdoors. Judy was able to get the job she wanted because she had a good math and science background in high school and a biology major in college. Judy's work keeps her in top physical shape, out of doors, and close to nature. On-the-job training has given her valuable experience in first aid, law enforcement, and public speaking. This exciting career field is very competitive and, for those who make it, the job satisfaction is great.

Learn what Judy's career is by matching the letters and your solutions below.

Complete the Percent Table; it will help you solve the problems.
Hint: 11% = 10% + 1%, 49% = 50% − 1%, etc.

Percent Table

What is 50% of 500?	250	
What is 25% of 500?	_____	
What is 10% of 500?	_____	
What is 5% of 500?	_____	
What is 1% of 500?	_____	
What is 50% of 600?	_____	
What is 25% of 600?	_____	
What is 10% of 600?	_____	
What is 5% of 600?	_____	
What is 1% of 600?	_____	

G: 6% of 500 is _____

D: 12% of 500 is _____

K: 19% of 500 is _____

M: 23% of 500 is _____

N: 65% of 500 is _____

B: 1% of 600 is _____

A: 3% of 600 is _____

F: 17% of 600 is _____

E: 24% of 600 is _____

P: 41% of 600 is _____

R: 49% of 600 is _____

___ ___ ___ ___   ___ ___ ___ ___ ___ ___

246   18   294   95   294   18   325   30   144   294

Katherine Donohue wanted a career where she wouldn't be sitting behind a desk all day, and she found one. Katherine does some exciting traveling in her work. One day she can be checking a clothing manufacturer's plant, the next day she may be at a food processing company, a stereo component company, or a perfume importer. Katherine has a quick mind, is good with math figures and problem solving. Her accurate and neat work habits along with the help of modern computers increase her company's efficiency and guarantee Katherine a stable job with a promising future. To get where she is today required a college education, a good understanding of math and business, and being able to pass a state exam.

To learn what Katherine's career is, match the letter to your estimate below. Estimate the answer to each problem.

A: $3.09 + $1.89 + $0.49 + $2.51

B: 10 pens at 39¢

C: $5.88 − $3.76

D: Three Frisbees at $1.89

E: 15 stamps at 20¢ each

F: $10 − $2.89

G: Change from $20 if you spend $4.95 and $1.76

I: Six liters at $1.49/liter

L: It takes _____ months to pay off $398.95 at $19.95 per month.

M: Cost to mail 12 packages at $2.76 each

N: Read 1 page/minute. 300 pages takes _____ hours.

O: 208 miles in 3 hours 57 minutes is about _____ miles per hour.

P: 600 bottles put in cases of 24 bottles is about _____ cases.

R: The average of 11, 12, 14, 18, 21 is about _____.

T: 40 is the average of _____, 40, and 50.

U: When stamps cost 19¢, how many for $2.00?

___	___	___	___	___	___	___	___	___
$2	$3	15	30	$9	$7	$9	$3	$6

___	___	___	___	___	___
25	10	$4	20	$9	$2

___	___	___	___	___	___	___	___	___	___
$8	$2	$2	50	10	5	30	$8	5	30

WHAT'S MY LINE?   Multiplication

In choosing her life work, Louise Scott followed in the career footsteps of her father and her grand-father. This traditionally glamorous and exciting career has allowed Louise to travel to such places as Tokyo, Hong Kong, and Sydney. With a strong math and science background, and a college degree, Louise was well prepared to make it through her intensive career training program.

In her work, Louise always has to be cool, calculating, quick thinking, and able to act intelligently in emergency situations. During her work, instruments relay nearly all the necessary information to Louise, but she is never able to relax and is always doing mental calculations as a back-up to her instruments. She is continually making mental notes and solving problems relating to air speed, air pressure, molecule compression, altitude, rate of fuel consumption, "dead reckoning" navigation, and more. Still, with all the concentration, calculations, and discipline that are so important in Louise's work, she loves the feeling of total control and total freedom she gets from her career.

Learn what Louise's career is by matching the letters and your solutions below:

Fill in the tables.

Solve these problems. In each case the number in the two spaces must be the same.

1 × 1	
2 × 2	
3 × 3	
4 × 4	
5 × 5	
6 × 6	
7 × 7	
8 × 8	
9 × 9	

10 × 10	
20 × 20	
30 × 30	
40 × 40	
50 × 50	
60 × 60	
70 × 70	
80 × 80	
90 × 90	

I: _____ × _____ = 1225

O: _____ × _____ = 361

D: _____ × _____ = 5329

E: _____ × _____ = 3249

V: _____ × _____ = 4225

T: _____ × _____ = 784

Y: _____ × _____ = 9216

L: _____ × _____ = 6724

U: _____ × _____ = 1681

N: _____ × _____ = 2809

P: _____ × _____ = 7744

J: _____ × _____ = 441

A: _____ × _____ = 11025

53   105   65   96   21   57   28   88   35   82   19   28

Plant Parenthood

1234567890123456789012345678901234567890123456789012345678901234567890123456789012345678901234567890123456789012345678901234567890

Skills
- *Applying probability reasoning*
- *Using fractions and percents*

Time
- *1–2 class periods*

Participants
- *Groups of 2 students*

Materials
- *Paper and pencils*
- *Scissors*
- *Rulers*
- *3" × 5" index cards in two colors; yellow for Plant I, white for Plant II (cut the cards in half)*
- *Paper bags*
- *Worksheet*

Scientific simulations allow exploration and organization of problems in many fields. In this activity, students consider the effects of dominant and recessive genes through a simulated inheritance activity. Knowledge about the rules of heredity and the role of chance in heredity are necessary in fields such as genetics (study of heredity), genetics counseling (counseling of parents who carry genes for abnormalities such as hemophilia or Tay-Sachs disease), agriculture, and animal husbandry.

Directions:

Give each pair of students half of a white card and half of a yellow card, a pair of scissors, and a ruler.

Students cut three 1" × 2½" strips from each half card.

Using the strips, each pair of students makes the Gene Cards according to the diagram below. Be careful to write the *Front* label on each strip, then turn it over and write the matching *Back* label.

PLANT I: Yellow Card

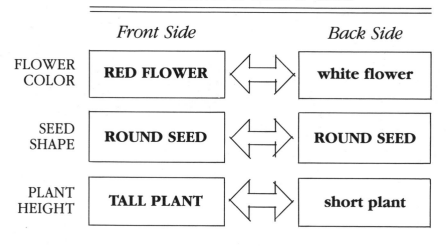

PLANT II: White Card

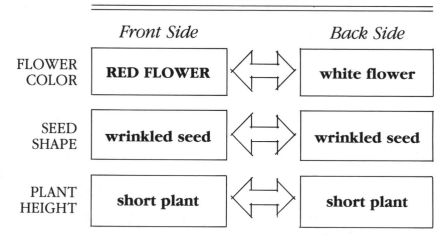

Explain to the students that each Gene Card represents the two genes or traits for a particular characteristic in a pea plant. The gene on the front of the card comes from one of the plant's parents, and the one on the back from the other parent.

Every plant has three gene cards in this activity, one for plant height, one for flower color, and one for seed shape.

Each characteristic has two types of genes or traits: TALL and short; RED and white; ROUND and wrinkled. Uppercase letters are used for dominant genes and lowercase letters for recessive genes.

Tell students the following rules of heredity:

a. A pea plant receives one gene for each characteristic at random from each parent.

b. A pea plant needs only *one* copy of a *dominant* gene (uppercase letters) in order to show that trait.

c. A pea plant needs *two* copies of a *recessive* gene (lowercase letters) to show that trait.

d. These rules will be used for the rest of this activity.

Ask the students to describe plants I and II. (Plant I is TALL with RED flowers and ROUND seeds. Plant II is short with RED flowers and wrinkled seeds.)

Apply these rules to see what one characteristic (say flower color) might look like in one offspring of Plants I and II. Shake the two flower color cards in the paper bag, and pour them onto the table. Look at the traits that are face up. Decide what trait will show in the offspring based on these traits.

Example:

Plant I   Plant II   Offspring

RED flower × white flower ⟹ RED flower

Repeat several times.

Simulate offspring of Plants I and II.

Before they begin the simulation, ask the students to describe the plants they think will result from the crosses. Each prediction should have a trait for plant height, flower color, and seed shape. Write the predictions on scratch paper.

113

Have each pair of students place one set of white and yellow gene cards (6 cards) in a paper bag. Shake the bag thoroughly and dump the gene cards onto the table. The genes that land face up will determine the traits of one offspring.

Match the traits that are showing for each characteristic, using a yellow one from plant I and a white one from Plant II.

Use the rules of heredity (above) to determine the appearance of this offspring. For example, if the following traits turn up:

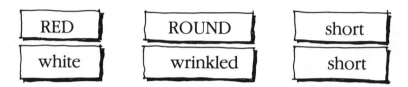

the offspring will be a short plant with RED flowers and ROUND seeds.

Make a chart to record these characteristics. List the plant height first, then flower color and seed shape:

	Plant Height	Flower Color	Seed Shape
1st offspring			
2nd offspring			
.			
.			
.			

Repeat this simulation until the appearance of 10 offspring has been determined.

Have each pair of students find the *percent* of their plant offspring with each trait: TALL, short, RED, white, etc. Then find these percents for the whole class. Compare the results of the simulation with the predictions. Discuss why the results might have occurred.

To determine why the results occur, analyze the probability of each trait occurring by completing the tables on the worksheet.

Example:

Plant Height

Possible Gene Combinations and Offspring:

Plant I

		TALL	short
Plant II	short	TALL × short TALL	short × short short
	short	TALL × short TALL	short × short short

The table has 4 sections. In 2 out of 4 sections the offspring will be TALL, so we say the probability of a TALL offspring from crossing Plant I and II is 2/4 or 1/2 or 50%. How does this compare with the simulated results?

What is the probability of a short offspring? How does this compare with the simulated results?

Have the students fill in the tables for Flower Color and Seed Shape and answer the questions on the worksheet. *Note:* Remind the students to change the probability fractions to percent to compare the probabilities with the results from the simulated cross.

Note that the tables give the *probability* of each trait. A probability of 1/2 for a TALL plant does not mean that exactly half of the plants from any simulation (or in real life) will be TALL, just that, when you look at a large number of crosses, approximately half will be TALL.

Extensions:

Determine what the parents of Plant I and Plant II might have looked like. To do this look at the genes the plant has for each characteristic. For example, Plant I has one RED flower gene from one parent and a white flower gene from the other. The parent that contributed the RED gene must have RED flowers. It could have a (RED, RED) pair of genes or a (RED, white) pair. The parent that contributed the white gene could have either white or RED flowers because it could have had either a (white, RED) or (white, white) pair of genes for flower color.

PLANT PARENTHOOD

Gene Combinations and Offspring Traits

Fill in all four sections of each table to find out all possible combinations of genes when you cross Plant I with Plant II.

PLANT HEIGHT

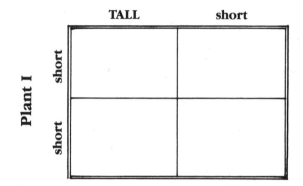

There are 2 traits for plant height in this cross: TALL and short.
Two of the 4 boxes produce a TALL plant.
We say the probability of a TALL plant is 2/4 = 1/2 or 50%.
How many of the 4 boxes produce a short plant? _____
What is the probability of a short plant?
_____ = _____%

FLOWER COLOR

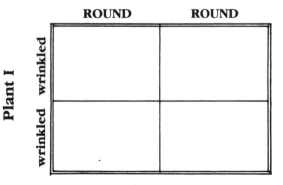

How many boxes result in a RED flower?
What is the probability of a RED flower in this cross? _____ = _____%
How many boxes result in a white flower?
What is the probability of a white flower?
_____ = _____%

SEED SHAPE

How many of the boxes resulted in ROUND seeds? _____
What is the probability of a ROUND seed from this cross? _____ = _____%
How many of the boxes resulted in wrinkled seeds? _____
What is the probability of a wrinkled seed?
_____ = _____%

HOW DO THESE RESULTS COMPARE WITH YOUR SIMULATION?

Do You Want To Be an Engineer?

1234567890123456789012345678901234567890123456789012345678901234567890123456789012345678901234567890123456789012345678901234567890

This questionnaire activity is designed to inform students about the characteristics that lead to success in engineering occupations, as well as in many other careers.

Directions:

Have the students number a sheet of paper from 1 to 20, as if for a true-false test or a spelling test.

Read each question aloud, with students writing down "yes" or "no" beside the number of the question.

After completing the questionnaire, read aloud each portion of the scoring directions. Discuss the questions for each section, or go back and read each question and discuss it individually.

This activity provides a unique opportunity for students to ask questions about the relationship between their own interests and possible future careers.

Please note that the intent of this activity is to inform and motivate students. The questions and the scoring are not scientifically designed.

Extensions:

1) If paper is not a problem, and you prefer each student to have a copy, this activity may be done as a written questionnaire, followed by discussion of the scoring and the questions.

2) The activity may also be used for homework or put into a learning center, since students can complete it without assistance.

3) Students may be interested in doing further research about a particular engineering field.

DO YOU WANT TO BE AN ENGINEER? Questionnaire

Answer

	Yes	No

1) When you were little, did you like taking things apart? . . . . ☐ ☐

2) Do you hate to do jigsaw puzzles? . . . . ☐ ☐

3) Do you feel that making an outline for a report is really important? . . . . ☐ ☐

4) Do you like working outdoors? . . . . ☐ ☐

5) Do you like working with a team of people? . . . . ☐ ☐

6) Is it hard for you to sketch a picture of something that others can recognize? . . . . ☐ ☐

7) Do you avoid playing strategy games, such as checkers or chess? . . . . ☐ ☐

8) Can you follow complicated directions? . . . . ☐ ☐

9) Do you like to travel to places that are not famous for scenery? . . . . ☐ ☐

10) Do you like to do projects with your hands, such as carving, macrame, or building models? . . . . ☐ ☐

11) Do you groan when you have to do the word problems in math? . . . . ☐ ☐

12) Can you write out detailed instructions for doing something? . . . . ☐ ☐

13) Do you think you would like using computers? . . . . ☐ ☐

14) When you look at a plan for something (like a model or a sewing pattern) do you have trouble imagining what it will look like? . . . . ☐ ☐

15) Do you like to have somebody tell you the answer to a problem before you have had a chance to figure it out? . . . . ☐ ☐

16) Would you rather study alone than with friends? . . . . ☐ ☐

17) Do you often think there must be a better way to build something? . . . . ☐ ☐

18) Do you have trouble reading a map? . . . . ☐ ☐

19) When you have a question about something, do you usually try to look it up in a dictionary or an encyclopedia? . . . . ☐ ☐

20) Do you like to give talks in front of the class? . . . . ☐ ☐

To find out the different skills that engineers use, look at each of the topics below and find out how you scored.

Technology and Mechanical Aptitude. See questions 1, 10, 13, and 17.
A majority of these questions answered with a yes shows mechanical aptitude. An engineer is sure to have a need for computers. It's also helpful to have confidence when it comes to taking things apart or putting them together. And, of course, thinking of better ways to build things might be part of your job. To develop these skills, practice working with puzzles, tools, and mechanical objects.

Spatial Visualization. See questions 2, 6, 14, and 18.
If you answered a majority of these questions with a no, you have good spatial skills. Jigsaw puzzles, drawing accurate pictures, visualizing rooms or models, and reading maps are indications of good spatial abilities. Your skills can be sharpened with practice.

Organization and Carefulness. See questions 3, 8, 12, and 19.
Do you work with care, plan ahead, and organize? For these questions, a majority answered with a yes shows good organization skills. An engineer is usually the basic organizer of a project and has to direct people, see that every detail is correctly done, and stay with the job until it is done to see that things go right. To practice writing out clear instructions, try using outlines or flow charts.

Problem Solving. See questions 2, 7, 11, and 15.
Engineers need to develop strategies and techniques for problem solving and the ability to keep trying until the problem is solved in the best way possible. If you answered these questions with a no, you are a good problem solver. To develop problem-solving skills, try all sorts of games, puzzles and "thinking" activities. Concentrate on *how* you are solving the problem or playing the game, so you can do it better next time.

Your Working Environment. See questions 4, 5, 9, 16, and 20.
These questions ask how you feel about your working environment. There are no right or wrong answers for an engineer, who may work alone or with others, indoors or outdoors, may travel or stay in one place, may have to appear in public or work out in the field or in an office. You might want to read about different kinds of engineers to find the one you like best.

Going to the Workforce

1234567890123456789012345678901234567890123456789012345678901234567890123456789012345678901234567890123456789012345678901234567890

Skills
- *Ordering*
- *Working cooperatively*
- *Estimating*
- *Decision making*

Time
- *20–30 minutes*

Participants
- *Groups of 3–5 students*

Materials
- *One Ranking Sheet for each student, and another one for each group of 3–5*

Students learn the minimum amount of math courses required to enter various occupations.

Directions:

Hand out the Ranking Sheets listing the ten occupations. Briefly discuss the type of work done in each of these fields. What is the minimum amount of high school and undergraduate college math a student must take to enter one of these careers? (*Not* how much math used in the career.) The answers will be scored against information given in the table on page 122. Statistics and computer science courses have been counted as mathematics.

Working Alone: The student's task is to rank the 10 jobs listed according to how much math a student is required to take in college and high school, starting with first year algebra. Place a number 1 by the job title which requires the most math, number 2 by the one which requires the next most math, and so on through number 10, which requires the least math.

Working in Small Groups: After students have completed the task, have them form groups of 3–5. Give each group a blank Ranking Sheet. They now have a second opportunity to rank the amount of math required for these occupations. This time they will be working with a small group of people, and the group will be asked to reach a consensus on each item. A decision process is most productive if it can make use of the resources of the group and resolve conflicts in a creative manner.

When the groups are finished, read the answers and have one member of each group score the group ranking. Individuals can score their own sheets for comparison with the group.

To score: Take the absolute value of the difference between the correct ranking and the one the group has given; that is, subtract then drop any negative signs.

Example:

	group answer	correct answer	difference
electrical engineer	4	1	3
chemist	2	6	4

Add all the differences for a total score. The lower the score, the more accurate the ranking.

Discussion: Ask whether any individual had a lower score than the group score. Discuss the dynamics within a group. Discuss the actual amount of math needed for each occupation. Discuss how math requirements have increased because of development in technology, such as computers.

Extensions:

1) Discuss the math and science courses the students should take in high school in order to pursue the careers of their choice.

2) Students can research the amount of math needed for other occupations.

3) Students can check the local colleges' math requirements for various majors. These will probably differ from this answer sheet.

4) Students can research what people do in the careers on the list and in any others that interest them. The *Occupational Outlook Handbook* is a good place to start.

Years of Math Required in:

Career	H.S.	College	Rank
electrical engineer	3*	4	1
astronomer	3	3	2
geologist	3	2⅔	3
biophysicist	3	2	4
business administration	3	1⅔	5
chemist	3	1⅓	6
architect	3	⅔	7
field biologist	3	⅓	8
draftsperson	2	½	9
electrician	1	0	10

*Three years of high school math implies that trigonometry is taught during the same year as second year algebra.

GOING TO THE WORKFORCE   Ranking Sheet

Rank the 10 occupations according to how many math courses a student must take in order to enter that field. Place number 1 by the job title which requires the most math courses, number 2 by the one requiring the next most math, and so on through number 10, which requires the least amount of math.

	Your Answer	Catalog Answer	Difference	
biophysicist	_____	_____	_____	
business administration	_____	_____	_____	
field biologist	_____	_____	_____	
electrician	_____	_____	_____	
draftsperson	_____	_____	_____	
electrical engineer	_____	_____	_____	
geologist	_____	_____	_____	
astronomer	_____	_____	_____	Total
architect	_____	_____	_____	Score
chemist	_____	_____	_____	_____

- ✂

Name:

GOING TO THE WORKFORCE   Ranking Sheet

Rank the 10 occupations according to how many math courses a student must take in order to enter that field. Place number 1 by the job title which requires the most math courses, number 2 by the one requiring the next most math, and so on through number 10, which requires the least amount of math.

	Your Answer	Catalog Answer	Difference	
biophysicist	_____	_____	_____	
business administration	_____	_____	_____	
field biologist	_____	_____	_____	
electrician	_____	_____	_____	
draftsperson	_____	_____	_____	
electrical engineer	_____	_____	_____	
geologist	_____	_____	_____	
astronomer	_____	_____	_____	Total
architect	_____	_____	_____	Score
chemist	_____	_____	_____	_____

Math Used in Jobs

1234567890123456789012345678901234567890123456789012345678901234567890123456789012345678901234567890123456789012345678901234567890

Skills
- *Ordering*
- *Decision making*
- *Working cooperatively*
- *Estimating*

Time
- *20–30 minutes*

Participants
- *Groups of 3–5 students*

Materials
- *One Ranking Sheet for each student and another one for each group of 3–5*

This activity will provide students with some answers to the frequently asked question, "When are we ever gonna have to use this?"

Directions:

Students guess which math skills are used most often in occupations. Explain to the students that the information was gathered by interviewing one hundred people in 100 different jobs to determine what kind of mathematics they actually use in their work. The 100 occupations are listed on the Ranking Sheet. Hand out the Ranking Sheets listing the 10 math skills.

Working Alone: Each student's task is to rank the 10 math skills listed according to how many occupations use this skill. Place number 1 by the math skill people mentioned that they used most often, number 2 by the skill used second most frequently, and so on through number 10, which is the math skill used the least.

Working in Small Groups: After the students have completed the task, have them form groups of 3–5. Give each group a blank Ranking Sheet. They now have a second opportunity to rank these math skills. This time they will be working with a small group of people, and the group will be asked to reach a consensus on each item. A decision process is most productive if it can make use of the resources of the group and resolve conflicts in a creative manner.

When the groups are finished, read the answers and have one member of each group score the group ranking. Individuals can score their own sheets for comparison with the group.

To score: Take the absolute value of the difference between the correct ranking and the one the group has given; that is, subtract then drop any negative signs.

Example:

	group answer	correct answer	difference
Fractions	**2**	**5**	**3**

Add all the differences for a total score. The lower the score, the more accurate the ranking.

Discussion: Ask whether any individual had a lower score than the group score. Discuss the dynamics within the group. Discuss the actual occupations and how the math skills may be used in each occupation.

Extensions:

Have students interview their parents or people in various careers to find out what type of math they use in their field. Students can then make a similar activity based on the information they collected.

MATH USED IN JOBS • ANSWERS

Math Skill	% of the 100 jobs that use this skill	Rank
decimals	100	1
calculators	98	2
percent	97	3
estimation	89	4
fractions	88	5
averaging	83	6
ratio and proportion	77	7
statistical graphs	74	8
formulas	68	9
basic geometric concepts	63	10

For students in upper-level math courses, use the sheet which lists 50 occupations using more advanced math topics.

ANSWERS

Math Skill	% of the 50 jobs that use this skill	Rank
area/perimeter	72	1
angle measurement	70	2
coordinate graphing	68	3
linear equations	66	4
exponents/scientific notation	64	5
probability	54	6
Pythagorean theorem	52	7
circles	50	8
vectors	48	9
trigonometric functions	44	10

*This activity was developed from *When Are We Ever Gonna Have to Use This?* by Hal Saunders. The book is published by Dale Seymour Publications, P.O. Box 10888, Palo Alto, CA 94303.

MATH USED IN JOBS

Ranking Sheet

Rank the 10 math skills according to how many people in the following occupations said they used the skill. Place number 1 by the math skill used most often, number 2 by the skill used second most frequently, and so on through number 10, which is the math skill used the least.

Use of	Your Answer	Actual Answer	Difference
fractions			
basic geometric concepts			
calculators			
formulas			
decimals			
averaging			
ratio and proportion			
estimation			Total
per cent			Score
statistical graphs			

Occupations

Accountant
Accounting Systems Analyst
Administrator: Shopping Mall
Advertising Agent
Airline Passenger Service Agent
Airplane Mechanic
Airplane Pilot
Air Traffic Controller
Appraiser (Land)
Architect
Artist (Graphic)
Attorney
Auditor
Auto Mechanic
Bank Teller
Biologist (Environmental)
Carpenter
Carpet Cleaner
Cartographer
Chiropractor
Computer Programmer
Computer Systems Engineer
Contractor (General)
Controller (Hospital)
Counter Clerk (Building Materials)
Data Processor
Dentist
Dietician
Doctor (G.P.)
Drafter
Economist
Electrician
Electrical Engineer

Electronics Technician
(Civil) Engineer
(Electronics) Engineer
(Industrial) Engineer
(Petroleum) Engineer
Environmental Analyst
Farm Advisor
Fire Prevention Officer
Fire Fighter
Forestry Land Manager
Forestry Recreation Manager
Geologist (Environmental)
Highway Patrol Officer
Hydrologist
Income Tax Preparer
Insurance Agent
Insurance Claims Supervisor
Interior Decorator
Investment Counselor
Landscape Architect
Librarian
Machinist
Manager: Appliance Store
Manager: Temp. Employment Service
Marketing Rep. (Computers)
Masonry Contractor
Medical Lab Technician
Meteorologist
Motorcycle Sales and Repair
Navigator
Newspaper: Circulation
Newspaper: Production
Newspaper: Reporter

Nurse
Oceanographer (Biological)
Optician
Orthopedic Surgeon
Painting Contractor
Payroll Supervisor
Personnel Administrator
Pharmacist
Photographer
Physical Therapist
Plumber
Police Officer
Political Campaign Manager
Printer
Psychologist (Experimental)
Publishing: Order Manager
Publishing: Production Manager
Purchasing Agent
Radio Technician
Real Estate Agent
Roofer
Savings Counselor
Sheet Metal/Heating Specialist
Social Worker
Stock Broker
Surveyor
Technical Researcher
Title Insurance Officer
Travel Agent
T.V. Repair Technician
Urban Planner
Veterinarian
Waitress/Waiter
Wastewater Treatment Operator

MATH USED IN JOBS | Ranking Sheet

Rank the 10 math skills according to how many people in the following occupations said they used the skill. Place number 1 by the math skill used most often, number 2 by the skill used second most frequently, and so on through number 10, which is the math skill used the least.

Use of	Your Answer	Actual Answer	Difference
circles	_____	_____	_____
coordinate graphing	_____	_____	_____
probability	_____	_____	_____
area/perimeter	_____	_____	_____
trigonometric functions	_____	_____	_____
linear equations	_____	_____	_____
angle measurement	_____	_____	_____
vectors	_____	_____	_____
exponents/scientific notation	_____	_____	_____
Pythagorean theorem	_____	_____	_____

Total Score _____

Occupations

Airplane Mechanic
Airplane Pilot
Air Traffic Controller
Appraiser (Land)
Architect
Biologist (Environmental)
Cartographer
Chiropractor
Computer Programmer
Computer Systems Engineer
Dentist
Doctor (G.P.)
Drafter
Economist
Electrician
Electrical Engineer
Electronics Technician

(Civil) Engineer
(Electronics) Engineer
(Industrial) Engineer
(Petroleum) Engineer
Environmental Analyst
Farm Advisor
Forestry Land Manager
Forestry Recreation Manager
Geologist (Environmental)
Hydrologist
Landscape Architect
Machinist
Marketing Rep. (Computers)
Medical Lab Technician
Meteorologist
Navigator
Newspaper: Production

Oceanographer (Biological)
Pharmacist
Photographer
Plumber
Psychologist (Experimental)
Purchasing Agent
Radio Technician
Real Estate Agent
Sheet Metal/Heating Specialist
Surveyor
Technical Researcher
Title Insurance Officer
Travel Agent
Urban Planner
Veterinarian
Wastewater Treatment Operator

WOMEN IN CAREERS

Classify the Classified
Startling Statements
Who's Where in the Workforce
Women Scientists

Classify the Classified

1234567890123456789012345678901234567890123456789012345678901234567890123456789012345678901234567890123456789012345678901234567890

Skills
* *Tallying*
* *Computing percents*
* *Researching information from original sources*
* *Constructing charts and graphs*

Time
* *2 class periods*

Participants
* *Groups of 2 students*

Materials
* *Telephone book yellow pages: one phone book for every 2 students, usually available free from local telephone company. If local directories do not have a large enough sample, get books from the nearest metropolitan area. Students may bring borrowed books from home for one day.*
* *Worksheet A: Tally sheet (1 for each pair of students)*
* *Worksheet B: Chart of Classified Occupations which may be enlarged for a wall chart or used on an overhead projector (1 per class)*
* *Worksheet C: Graphing forms (1 for each student)*
* *Crayons or colored pens*

This is an investigation of the names of professional people listed in the telephone book "yellow pages" (or classified section) to find the relative number of males and females in some professions. Students will do research, then organize and interpret data, while learning about a variety of careers.

Some occupations that will probably be listed in your local telephone book:

* Accountant
* Architect
* Attorney
* Dentist
* Engineer: Civil, Consulting, Mechanical, Structural

* Optometrist
* Physician: Pediatrician, Psychiatrist, General Practice, Surgeon
* Veterinarian

Directions:

Tell the students that they will use the yellow pages of the phone book to look up several professions. By identifying first names as male or female, they can calculate approximately what percent are men and what percent are women in these professions.

• Are there the same number of men and women in most occupations?

Help the class generate a list of possible occupations that might be found in the yellow pages. Write the list on the chalkboard. Have a reliable student checking the list against the phone book as occupations are listed. Look for categories that list individual names.

• Are secretaries and carpenters listed in the yellow pages?
• What do you find when you look up electrician?
• Does the list of gardeners include names of many individuals?

When the list is complete (see occupation list above) and matches the phone book, assign each pair of students an occupation from the chalkboard. List each pair's occupation on Worksheet B Chart, column 1. (Chalkboard or overhead.)
• Which occupation do you think will have the most names?

Have the students estimate what percent of the people in each occupation are male and what percent are female. Let the pair that has the occupation make the estimate.
• Are there more men or women in this occupation?
• Have you ever seen a woman doing this job? A man?

Record the estimates on Worksheet B Chart. Enter the estimate for females in column 4 and the estimate for males in column 7.
• Do the two percent figures for the occupation add up to 100%?

Distribute phone books. Be sure estimates are made before phone books are passed out.

Discuss tallying with the students, if needed.
• What does a tally show?
• Who really uses tallies?

Tally part of a list with the class to make sure the instructions are clear. Arrive at rules for including or excluding any given name. An overhead projection of a phone book page may be helpful.
• Is "Leslie" a man's name or woman's name?
• Are "Marion" and "Marian" the same?
• What about an initial?
• Do we need to keep a record of names we don't use?
• Do we need a total count?

Have the students locate their occupation in the phone book. One student reads the first names from that section while the second student makes a tally count on their Worksheet A.

When tallying is complete, the students compute percents on the tally sheet, following the instructions given.

After the students have entered information from the tally sheets onto Worksheet B Chart, review the results.
• Were estimates close to actual figures?

Make a graph of the occupations, showing male and female percents. There are many ways to present this information in graphic form. Depending on student experience, you may want to allow students to create their own graphs or you may have them complete the bar graph begun on Worksheet C.

After the graphs have been completed, discuss the meaning of the graph in relation to the statistics.

CLASSIFY THE CLASSIFIED   Worksheet A

Tally Sheet

Date _____   Occupation _____

Student Names _____   _____

Source of Information _____

Tally of Female Names   *Tally of Male Names*

Summary: ## Enter on Worksheet B (Chart)

Total number of tallies, male and female   _____   Enter tally total in Column 2

Number of names identified as female   _____   Enter in Column 3

Percent of names identified as female   _____ %   Enter in Column 5

Number of names identified as male   _____   Enter in Column 6

Percent of names identified as male   _____ %   Enter in Column 8

Chart of Classified Occuations

Location _____

		Female			Male		
Occupation 1	Total Count 2	Tally Count 3	Est. % 4	Local % 5	Tally Count 6	Est. % 7	Local % 8

Graph of Yellow Page Occupations

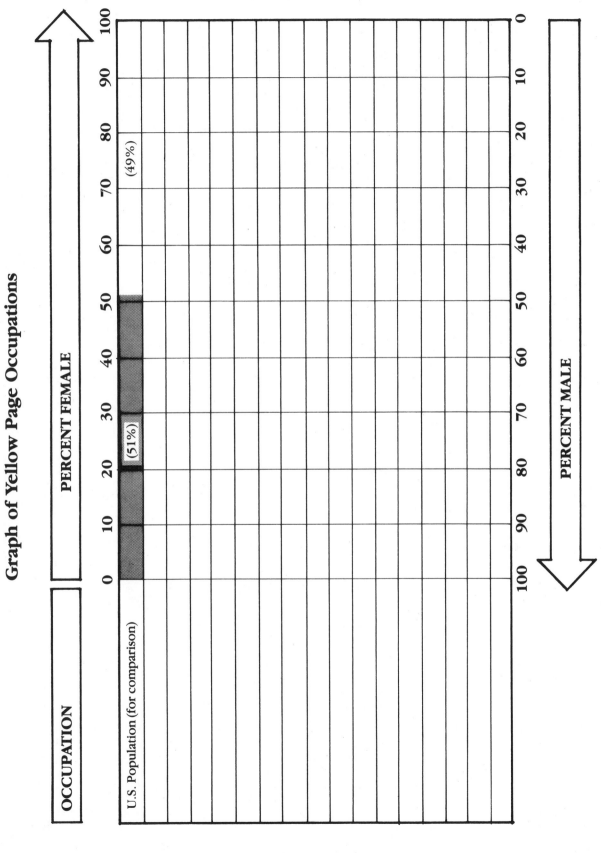

DIRECTIONS: Write the name of the occupation in the left column. Make a line on the bar space under the number that represents the percent of females (numbers at the top of the chart) in this occupation. Color the bar space from zero to that line with crayon, colored pen, or pencil. Color the rest of the bar space another color. The second color represents the percent of males in this occupation. (Read the percent from the bottom of the chart.)

Startling Statements

1234567890123456789012345678901234567890123456789012345678901234567890123456789012345678901234567890123456789012345678901234567890

Skills
- *Averaging*
- *Estimating*

Time
- *20–45 minutes*

Participants
- *Groups of 4 or 5 students*

Materials
- *3 or 4 Startling Statement sheets, cut into strips, with 1 question on each strip*
- *Scotch tape*

This awareness activity increases students' knowledge of participation by men and women in different occuations.

Directions:

Tell the students that many occupations require special training but that most jobs are open to both men and women who are qualified. The students will estimate the current status of men and women in several occupations and the related consequences of that status.

Scotch tape one question on each student's back. Several students may have the same question, depending on class size. Have the students stand, walk around the room, and ask 5 other students what the answer is to the question on their back. Once they have 5 answers, they should sit down and find the average and range of their 5 answers.

Read a question and have the students who had that question give you their answer and range. Give the correct answer. Continue until all of the questions have been answered.

Extensions:

Have each student research and write a startling question; make sure that they include their source of information.

Answers to Startling Statements

(Letter in parentheses indicates source.)

1. 13.4% (a)		**5.** 4.3% (a)		**9.** $12,600 (b)	
2. 98.7% (a)		**6.** 4% (a)		**10.** 4% (c)	
3. 13% (a)		**7.** $26,628 (b)			
4. 94% (a)		**8.** 99.1% (a)			

Sources

a) *Employment and Unemployment: A Report on 1980.* U.S. Department of Labor, Bureau of Labor Statistics, Washington, D.C., Special Labor Force Report 244, Table 23, April 1981.

b) *Manpower Comments.* Scientific Manpower Commission, Washington, D.C., Vol. 18, No. 1, January-February 1981.

c) *Facing the Future: Education and Equity for Females and Males.* Council of Chief State School Officers and National Association of State Boards of Education, 400 North Capitol Street, N.W., Suite 379, Washington, D.C., December 1980.

STARTLING STATEMENTS

1. What percent of employed doctors are women?

2. What percent of employed electricians are men?

3. What percent of working lawyers are women?

4. What percent of employed architects are men?

5. Women are 98% of employed dental assistants; what percent of practicing dentists are women?

6. Women are 52% of the U.S. population. What percent are they of the U.S. engineering force?

7. What is the average yearly salary offer to a student with a 1981 bachelor's degree in petroleum engineering?

8. What percent of secretarial jobs are held by women?

9. What is the average yearly salary offer to a student with a 1981 bachelor's degree in the humanities?

10. Women are 51% of secondary school teachers; what percent are they of secondary school principals?

Who's Where in the Workforce

1234567890123456789012345678901234567890123456789012345678901234567890123456789012345678901234567890123456789012345678901234567890

Skills
- *Estimating*
- *Converting percents to degrees of a circle*
- *Making a circular graph*

Time
- *1–2 class periods*

Participants
- *Individual or groups of 2 students*

Materials
- *Unlined paper*
- *Rulers*
- *Protractors*
- *Optional: Compasses*

Information on the composition of the workforce in the United States gives students a realistic view of their own opportunities to enter some careers. Circle graphs are used as a way of organizing information.

Directions:

Write on the chalkboard the following categories for the U.S. workforce.

1980 U.S. Workforce	%
Business	_____
Professional/Technical	_____
Health/Medical	_____
Industry/Transportation/Farms	_____
Service	_____
Communication/Art/Design/Glamour	_____

Ask the students to estimate what percent of the 1980 U.S. Workforce works in each category.

When the students have completed the task, give the correct answers.

1980 U.S. Workforce

Business   35%
Managers (11%)
Sales workers (6%)
Clerks/Secretaries (18%)

Professional/Technical   11%
Scientists/Technicians (6%)
Teachers/Social Workers/
Librarians (5%)

Health/Medical   7%
Doctors/Dentists/
   Veterinarians (3%)
Nurses/Medical Assistants (4%)

Industry/Transportation/Farms   33%
Skilled craft workers (12%)
Operatives/Truck drivers/
   Machine operators (14%)
Farmers/Laborers (7%)

Service   13%
Police Officers/Firefighters/
   Waitresses/Beauticians

Communication/Art/Design/
Glamour   1%
Entertainers/Models/
Professional athletes/
Fashion designers

Discuss the differences between the students' estimates and the actual percentages.

Next, students are to take the information on the board and make their own circle graph displaying the data. A compass, the protractor, or anything circular can be used for making the circle.

To prepare students for this part of the activity, review the skill of reading and using a protractor. The students will also need to understand the relationship between *degrees* in a circle and *percent* of degrees in a circle (e.g. 50% of the degrees in a circle is 180°). It may help if the students convert each of the given percentages to degrees before beginning to plan the graph.

Extensions:

Discuss which job categories might be expanding in the future and which ones might decline. Have students pick the work categories they feel they may enter in the future. Write all the choices on the board and change to percents. Graph this information in a circle graph. How does it compare to the U.S. Workforce? Will it be more competitive to enter some occupations than others? Are the career choices of the students realistic compared to the actual jobs that may be available in that field?

Source:

Employment and Unemployment During 1980. U.S. Department of Labor, Bureau of Labor Statistics, Washington, D.C.

Women Scientists

Skills
- *Reading*
- *Memorizing*
- *Recognizing patterns*

Time
- *1 class period*

Participants
- *Groups of 3–5 students*

Materials
- *36 playing cards for Women Scientists game*

For centuries, women scientists have been unknown to most people, and their names and histories are unfamiliar. In this activity, students acquire knowledge of women of historical importance in the scientific professions.

Preparation:

Duplicate and cut one set of 36 cards for each group of 3–5 students. Form student groups for a typical card game.

Directions:

Women Scientists is a "Go Fish" kind of card game made up of three information cards on each of 12 women in history who made contributions to scientific and technical fields. The object of the game is to lay down the most "books"; each book consists of three cards that are about the same woman scientist.

In each group, a student shuffles the cards and stacks them, face down, on the table. Each player in turn draws a card, reads it aloud, and keeps it in his or her hand. When a player whose turn has come has a card which he or she remembers is similar to one held by another player, the player whose turn it is may ask for the card before drawing. If the request is correct, the card (or cards) must be given to the requesting player and the player may continue to ask for cards. If the request is incorrect, the player asked replies, "Go take another science course." The requesting player then draws from the pile. If the card just asked for is drawn, the player gets another draw.

Each card that is drawn from the stack must be read aloud before the player places the card among the cards in his or her hand. Any player who notices that another player forgot to read the card may claim it, read it, and keep it as part of his or her hand. Players may lay down any complete books they have at the end of their turn. The play continues until all cards are used. The player with the most books wins.

Ellen Swallow did outstanding work in chemical analysis.	Contributions to physics, especially in the area of sound and elasticity, were made by Sophie Germain.	To discourage Sophie Germain from studying late at night, her parents took away her sources of heat and light.
A famous mathematician tried to get Emmy Noether a place on the faculty of a German university saying, "After all, we are a university, not a bathing establishment."	Emmy Noether altered the course of algebra by her work.	In 1900 Emmy Noether, mathematician, was one of two women among the 1,000 students enrolled in her university.
The first woman ever invited to join the American Academy of Sciences was Maria Mitchell, astronomer.	In 1847, Maria Mitchell sighted the first comet ever discovered by telescope.	Maria Mitchell, astronomer, started the association for the advancement of women in 1873.
Since women were not admitted, Marie Curie could not attend the University of Warsaw.	An outstanding black woman space scientist, Katherine Johnson, has worked on spacecraft such as the earth resources satellite.	Sophie Germain worked in number theory, and won several prizes for her work in mathematical physics.

Mary Somerville, mathematician, developed the beginning steps toward the concept of conservation of energy.

The prediction of the existence of the planet Neptune was made possible by Mary Somerville's work.

The interconnection of physical forces is founded on Mary Somerville's work.

The first Native American woman doctor in the United States was Susan La Flesche.

Susan La Flesche was the daughter of a chief of the Omaha Indian tribe.

After graduating from medical school, Susan La Flesche returned to practice medicine among her people, the Omaha Indian tribe.

Chien Shiung Wu (Chee en She ung Woo) was promoted to full professor of physics at Columbia University and became the seventh woman member of the U.S. National Academy of Sciences.

When there were no female students allowed at Princeton, Chien Shiung Wu (Chee en She ung Woo) was invited to teach nuclear physics there in 1943.

Chien Shiung Wu (Chee en She ung Woo) designed an experiment that helped earn the Nobel Prize in Physics in 1957.

Because she was a woman, Sonya Kovalevski was denied admission to the French Academy of Sciences.

In 1874, after producing outstanding work in mathematics, Sonya Kovalevski received her Doctorate from the University of Gottingen in Germany.

Sonya Kovalevski made important contributions to the study of the shape and behavior of Saturn's rings.

Margaret Mead wrote *Coming of Age in Samoa* and other studies of South Sea societies.

Margaret Mead, anthropologist, studied primitive and modern societies.

By studying other cultures, Margaret Mead helped us to understand our own culture.

Even though she had discovered radium and polonium, Marie Curie was refused admission to the French Academy of Sciences.

The first person in the world ever to win two nobel prizes was Marie Curie.

Rebecca Lee received her medical degree in 1864 from the New England Female Medical College.

After the Civil War, Rebecca Lee returned to the South and established her medical practice in Richmond, Virginia.

The first black woman doctor in the United States was Rebecca Lee.

Katherine Johnson was a recipient of a group achievement award presented by NASA's Lunar Spacecraft and Operations Team.

Katherine Johnson, space scientist, studied the mathematics and physics of spacecraft travel.

Devoting her life to studying and teaching about healthful environments, Ellen Swallow popularized the word ecology.

The first woman admitted to M.I.T. was Ellen Swallow, but she was denied the Doctorate in Chemistry there because she was a woman.